Through the Belly of the *Beast* and Back

Through the Belly of the *Beast* and Back

My Life In Foster Care

TITANIA D. GRACE

iUniverse, Inc.
Bloomington

Through the Belly of the Beast and Back
My Life in Foster Care

iUniverse books may be ordered through booksellers or by contacting:

iUniverse
1663 Liberty Drive
Bloomington, IN 47403
www.iuniverse.com
1-800-Authors (1-800-288-4677)

ISBN: 978-1-4759-4693-2 (sc)
ISBN: 978-1-4759-4695-6 (hc)
ISBN: 978-1-4759-4694-9 (ebk)

Library of Congress Control Number: 2012916127

Printed in the United States of America

iUniverse rev. date: 10/25/2012

Contents

Author's Note

Writing this book was dear to my heart, necessary and yet terrifying. There were in fact several times when I considered not completing this book out of fear of what might come. Sometimes I worried about remembering certain details of my childhood, particularly the events leading up to and following being in foster care. Other times I feared what would come from sharing personal accounts of the foster children I had worked with and of what this might mean for my career. There were even times that I cried while writing this book and had to stop for days at a time before I could return to it. However, I felt compelled to write this in light of what I had seen happening to the kids and teens in foster care. From the stories I heard from other social workers to the heartfelt accounts from the kids and teens that experienced atrocities first hand, I knew that I couldn't keep my silence. Working with foster kids and teens also opened my eyes to a world that I had once personally known but had tried to separate from my professional role as a social worker. I had tried to compartmentalize and neatly pack away my personal experiences of growing up in foster care. I never thought that working within the child welfare system would bring me face to face with the worst memories of my own childhood. I certainly didn't believe that it would change me the way it has over the past few years. Yet, working with foster children and adolescents ignited something inside of me that had been dormant for the past few years. It ignited something that had almost been silenced from the hopelessness that I had started to feel from working within the child welfare system. The treatment of foster children and youth was often jaw dropping, mind-boggling and left me feeling dazed. It seemed in many regards like it became a different dimension. In fact I often joked with colleagues of mine that it was like being an episode of the Twilight Zone. It was like we were in a different world all together where the rules of this world seemed suspended from reality. Yet I had to do my best to make sense of a world that many kids and teens come to see as their reality. I had to try with everything I had left inside of me to instill a sense of hope, even when I had lost a great deal of hope from my daily struggles within the system. Writing this book became my mission to give those children in foster care a voice that had become silenced after the many losses and battles that they endured in their short time in this world. I also wanted to voice the concerns that I among plenty of my social work colleagues have expressed during those afternoons we ate lunch together. Thus, writing this book became a mission to bring these issues out into the forefront in hopes that greater discussions for change can begin.

Acknowledgements

To All of You with Love and Appreciation

This book is dedicated to all of the foster kids who have struggled to have their voices heard and who fight to keep hope for a better future in a system that tests their resiliency every day. I am also dedicating this book to the social workers and other child welfare workers who wholeheartedly fight to repair the broken parts of the foster care system.

I must also extend a special thanks to three women who have taught me so much about life, love and giving back, my grandmother Mary, my mother Vanessa, and my mentor Gail.

Last but not least, special thanks to my friend Jason D. Boroff for supporting me in following my dream of writing this book. To my dear friend Hans-Martin Jaeger, who continues to show me what true friendship is. Thanks for providing your support and for editing this book. To Cecil Burger, the Graphic Designer and Photographer for this book, who visually helped me to tell my story with beauty and grace. May yours and Bill's photography and graphic design company *Once Upon a HoneyBee* blossom well beyond your dreams.

Introduction

The events that led me to write this book were so compelling and urgent that I found myself pushing harder than I had ever pushed to get my thoughts down on paper. In many ways this book is a tell all. *Through the Belly of the Beast and Back: My Life in Foster Care* is filled with my encounters and life changing experiences with a harsh system that, while created to protect children, ends up causing additional loss and trauma as they move through it.

Throughout this book I share my personal experiences and the heartfelt accounts of the treatment I witnessed of several children I have worked with while working as a social worker for a program within a well-known social service agency. The program was designed for children in foster care that have emotional disturbances, developmental disabilities and/or are medically fragile. The goal of the program is to keep children within the community as opposed to having them hospitalized or sent to residential treatment facilities. It was during this time that I met with the children within their foster homes, at agencies, at their schools and other places within the community. During this period, in addition to working with the children enrolled in the program, I also worked with some of the biological parents who had not lost their parental rights. It was also during this time that I worked closely with several foster care agencies alongside case workers, case associates, behavioral specialists, and fellow social workers.

This book not only reveals the twisted experiences of the children and adolescents whose lives I have seen torn into shreds, but also my personal experiences of growing up in foster care. Overall, there are many underhanded things that I have seen take place with children in foster care that strip away their self-esteem and in many ways any hopes of having a healthy childhood. Yet there are people who stand to profit from their many losses. On the other hand, I have seen social workers and other child welfare workers who work hard to make changes to the foster care system. Even so, the child welfare system has a way of pulling us in only to spread us so thin that we have very little to give toward change. Instead I have seen first-hand how the system makes us feel powerless to make the many changes needed, and how we often become so burnt out that we switch agencies when there is so much to be done at the agencies that we leave.

Chapter One

The Ridiculousness of Foster Care

My experiences working within child welfare, in particular my work with foster care agencies have left an even more bitter taste in my mouth than my worst experiences of growing up in foster care. What I have witnessed as a social worker haunts me like the memories of my childhood traumas. Sometimes the images from my past blend together in a blurry mixture of horrible vivid scenes. The awkwardness, the anxiety, the fears, the instability and the many losses, they at times all get lumped together. Sometimes it's so hard to take in that I shut off. Other times I envision that what I experienced is distant. Likewise, I often do my best to think of the horrendous treatment I have witnessed of the children in foster care as being distant. As if thinking of both harsh realities as distant memories will help ease the impact. Other times I have tried to envision what I have seen, heard and experienced as a fictional movie. After all while there are plenty of fictional movies that can invoke powerful emotions, there is also a part of you that realizes that it's not real. You may even feel a little silly after being afraid or after crying about certain scenes. But the traumas I have experienced during my childhood and the current state of the foster care system are real. So real that no matter how I try to see things, these experiences won't ever go away. Once you get taken into the system, it seems to hold a firm grip on you. It becomes so attached as if it's your own skin. You wear it because it's not something that you can easily get rid of. Over the past few years I've tried to deal with it and figure out ways to make it better from within. I've so desperately wanted to make changes to the broken system. It's hard not to want to make changes, when I continue to see more innocent children suffer and families being torn apart each day. For what, who wins, when so many people lose?

Meal ticket?

When I was a kid I heard stories of foster parents who got involved not because they cared about giving a child a good home, but because they saw a meal ticket. Perhaps it was their last resort, perhaps their dreams never got fully realized. Either way, there was often talk of people who saw foster children as just another way to add to their income. It was often easy to spot these types of people in a neighborhood because one day a kid or teen would appear in their home and stay longer than any visitor would stay. The newcomer would in fact stay longer than most relatives get to stay. Plus a new face in the neighborhood always got people talking. Other kids wanted to know who this person was, and the adults wanted to gossip about how this person got there and why they had stayed so long. It was almost like living in a small town where everyone knows your business. The younger kids often found out about the truth from the older kids, who often overheard the grown-ups talking about how this new person came about and why. Or perhaps some had been lucky enough to be a part of the conversation about this newcomer. Either way, somehow nearly everyone in the neighborhood would find out. Once it came out that a foster child was present, people would begin to talk about how different the neighbor's apartment would look. However, most of the time it seemed like the foster child didn't appear to be reaping the same financial benefits. In fact, while the neighbor would have large screen TVs, stereo systems that most people in the neighborhood only dreamt of, and of course new name brand clothes, the child would often have clothing that was second hand. Most of these children would stay around for what seemed like a season or two. Then all of a sudden they would be gone as if they were never there. Rumors of the kid running away or being too difficult would be talked about, especially during the weekend gossip. Then a new face would appear at the same neighbor's home within a few months; new face, but the same benefits were talked about regarding the foster parent. However, as a kid that was the only way of which I was aware that others could profit at the expense of foster children. I had no idea how financially motivated and lucrative the foster care system was for others.

Chapter Two

Big Business

From the foster parents that get involved based on what they see as easy money to the myriad of mental health providers working with these children, how do these children have a true shot at a healthy life? Everyone seems to be looking for ways to cash in on foster kids. I have seen one foster child have a case associate, a case planner, a behavioral specialist, a psychiatrist, and an individual therapist. On top of those providers, if the child is enrolled in other programs like the one I worked for, they will also have a health care integrator and waiver services provider(s). So, these children are expected to spend their free time with visits from all of the above providers and must be willing to express their feelings and anything else that is going on in their life. While each of these providers are typically paid by Medicaid, these children become less like people and more like products to profit from. Forget about privacy, everyone gets a piece of their lives. It appears that everyone wants them to expose more and more about their life in order to fill some chart or comply with some program mandate. Whether it's at home or at school, these children are expected to forget that they are children and instead become a piece of a money-making puzzle. The older children and teens often grow a great deal of mistrust and start to see each provider as just another part of the system that looks to take from them.

It gets to a point where nearly everything appears to be about numbers. At my last job with the program I worked for, it often felt like it was a numbers game. Instead of how many of these foster children we could help, the emphasis seemed to be placed on other factors.

There was instead a great amount of pressure regarding how many clients we could retain by not having parents dis-enroll their children from the program. My supervisor seemed less concerned about what was or wasn't accomplished during the visits and more with meeting the mandated two visits per month. It was always made crystal clear that we had to meet the mandated visits in order to ensure that we could bill Medicaid. Every month was a numbers game. There were even competitions between teams to see which supervisor's team could achieve 100% billing each month. While monetary prizes weren't given, there certainly was kudos expressed during staff meetings.

Yet, with the countless programs and appointments that these children have to keep, many of them become frustrated and non-compliant with services. Quite a few of the children and teens that I have worked with have expressed to me that they didn't feel that anyone was listening to how they felt about the amount of people they had to meet with each month. Out of frustration I have witnessed several of them deal with their perceived powerlessness by not being fully engaged, or at times with complete avoidance. I have seen the younger children typically show their resistance by only talking about on-the-surface topics, or by not wanting to participate in activities during their mandated visits. With teens I have noticed that many of them will completely avoid meeting with social workers by not arriving home for the time that the appointment was set for. Even when school visits are encouraged, many of the teens will avoid meeting by showing up late to school and at times not even attending school. Either way, it seems clear that they have a wall up.

Many of these children struggle with trust based on their experiences of neglect or abuse, often from those who were closest to them. The kids I have worked with have expressed that they feel let down and abandoned by their biological families as well as tossed around when their foster parents feel that they are too much to handle. So a new person may look like a new opportunity for them to be let down or abandoned by. It doesn't help that there is often a high turnover of workers within the child welfare system. As a social worker, in particular in my most recent work with children in foster care, I have realized that I need to address this concern from the beginning instead of having it be the elephant in the room. Firstly, I never assure them that I will always be their social worker. Secondly, I compare the change in child welfare providers to the change they have in teachers each year of school. What I emphasize is that while they may get new teachers each year, the change in teachers doesn't take away what they have learned from the previous year. I have found that children and teens not only appreciate my honesty, but that they are also open to seeing a different perspective of the issue of the high turnover of workers. However, even with that perspective, many of them still have to cope with the large number of workers they are expected to meet with on a regular basis.

Chapter Three

Too Many Providers, Too Little Time for Being a Kid: Something Must Be Wrong with Me

I often wonder how many of these children see themselves in a positive light, when the focus often seems to be on what's wrong with them. Day in and day out they are asked to work on what's wrong with them. Perhaps they feel what I used to, that something about them is broken and needs to be fixed. By the age of 11 many of them are very aware of their mental health diagnosis and have a vast number of providers in their life. They are led to believe that something is so wrong with them that they need several mental health providers to make them better. It is as if who they are isn't good enough and that they need an army of people to change them into something better. I wonder how much all of this affects their self-esteem. How do they see themselves after being prescribed an elaborate list of programs and mental health providers who are scheduled to see them at school, mental health clinics, hospitals, and even at home. From the constant flow and change of case workers, social workers and other providers in their lives, I worry about what their childhood memories will be filled with. When do they have time to just be children and teens? I mean if they have to be committed to doing things to better themselves, why not use the time to have them learn a foreign language, learn to play an instrument, travel, participate in programs that promote the arts or entrepreneurial and leadership skills? Yet instead they have to juggle their free time with one mental health provider after another and repeat their story over and over again to people who rarely ever stay in their lives.

Desiree

This reminds me of a young girl that I worked with who I will refer to as Desiree. Her qualifying mental health diagnosis for enrollment into the program was Adjustment Disorder with Depressed Mood, R/O Impulse Control, Oppositional Defiant Disorder, Physical Abuse of a Child; with R/O meaning that the other mental disorders hadn't been ruled out.

Desiree was a 14 year-old African American girl who had been in foster care for most of her life. She was bright, talented and full of potential. Yet she was also very self-conscious, self-critical and full of doubt. When we first met, she was very soft-spoken and incredibly quiet. It was as if she wanted to disappear into her soft spoken words and fade away, like her voice often did mid-conversation. When asked to describe her strengths, she initially couldn't think of anything. It took months for her to realize the wonderful qualities that I saw from the beginning. My heart went out to her, as I thought of how sad it was that this young girl couldn't think of anything positive when she thought of herself. Yet how could anyone blame her for not seeing how great she was, when most of her life was filled with tragedy, loss, instability, and an abundance of mental health services and providers trying to fix her? According to Desiree's chart, her biological mother had been killed shortly after the birth of Desiree's younger brother Sean. After her mother's death Desiree and her younger brother went to live with their maternal grandmother.

According to Desiree's records, their grandmother was informed that Desiree needed to be in therapy to cope with the loss of her mother. However, when the grandmother expressed that she felt that Desiree was too young to receive therapy, both Desiree and Sean were removed from their grandmother's home. After being removed from their grandmother's home both children were placed in a non-kinship foster home. While they were adopted by a couple, both siblings were later removed from this home due to reports of excessive corporal punishment by their adoptive mother. After this move, Desiree and her younger brother were forced to move into a different foster home where they remained for four years. However, after four years their foster mother failed to plan for the adoption of both siblings. According to Desiree's chart, Ms. Jarrod only wanted to adopt Desiree. So Desiree and Sean were removed from Ms. Jarrod's home and sent to a new foster home with Ms. Carrington. However, according to the records, Desiree and Sean had physical altercations that resulted in Desiree being removed from this home. As a result, Desiree was temporarily placed at a crisis center for children until they felt she was stable enough for a new foster home. Her brother Sean was removed from the foster home of Ms. Carrington and was later sent to a residential treatment facility.

After being removed from Ms. Carrington's home, Desiree and Sean only saw each other during supervised visits at the facility where Sean lived. I wasn't Desiree's social worker at this time, so I can't say for sure what really happened during this period. Yet all of this seemed so hard for me to believe based on the love that Desiree often expressed when talking about Sean. I found myself often wondering how much of this was exaggerated or perhaps misunderstood. I mean all siblings fight, and both of them had plenty to be frustrated about. Plus when Desiree spoke of Sean, she often expressed a great deal of concern about him. Desiree often told me that she missed Sean and was worried about him being somewhere that she couldn't protect him. Desiree also told me of a biological aunt who had told her that she would adopt Desiree and Sean. Yet due to her aunt not submitting the necessary paperwork to the foster care agency to start the kinship foster home process, Desiree's hope for this didn't materialize during the time that I worked with her. Nonetheless, whenever this subject came up or when there were any updates regarding the possibility of her aunt getting custody of them, Desiree would express her desire for her and Sean to be reunited. So it was difficult for me to envision Desiree wanting to hurt Sean.

However, whatever the case was, Desiree's home and sense of security was disturbed once again due to accusations that she and Sean continued to fight. By the time that Desiree was 14, she had already been in five foster homes. When Desiree and I met, she was in her fifth foster home and had expressed to my first supervisor that she feared for her safety there. During a transfer meeting in which the previous health care integrator was providing Desiree's history to me, it was discussed that, following a meeting with Desiree and her foster mother, Desiree had asked to speak privately to my supervisor. During the conversation Desiree had told my supervisor that she was afraid of being in the foster home and wanted to leave the meeting with her. When my supervisor relayed this message to the social workers at the foster care agency, they claimed that Desiree was exaggerating. According to my supervisor and a waiver service provider manager present at that transfer meeting, this foster mother was verbally aggressive. She also seemed resistant to the program from the beginning and was more concerned about her hair appointment than scheduling a time for the health care integrator to visit the home. However, since it was my first week on the job, I wasn't sure about what all of this would mean or how things would transpire. Though, no matter how much they told me or how much I read about Desiree or her foster mother, I wanted to meet them before I formed an impression of them.

One month into working with Desiree, due to my supervisor relocating to a different state I received a new supervisor. While I won't say that my new supervisor didn't appear to care as much about Desiree's safety as my first supervisor, I will say that a great deal of emphasis was placed on being able to meet the mandated visits. Perhaps my new supervisor being new to this position and being on her six-month probationary period was the reason behind her not wanting to look deeper into what Desiree had previously communicated. Perhaps she just wanted to do whatever would create less waves. Whatever the case was, Desiree's feelings didn't seem to have the same sense of urgency. However, as time went on Desiree often confided in me that Ms. Grant allegedly threatened her. According to Desiree, she was told by Ms. Grant that if she got out of line, Ms. Grant's nieces would "jump her." However, my supervisor expressed that if Desiree was being abused, she would report the abuse to someone, but that I should keep an eye on things while working with Desiree. However, I felt uncomfortable about not exploring the alleged threats made by Desiree's foster mother Ms. Grant.

Finally my supervisor suggested that instead of discussing the alleged threats, we should follow up with the social workers at the foster care agency regarding Desiree expressing that she wanted to be removed from her current foster home. However, again they continued to express that Desiree was manipulative and that they didn't feel she was in danger. According to the behavioral specialist, Ms. Grant had another foster child in her home and the other child hadn't made any allegations of abuse against Ms. Grant. So Desiree's cries for help were not looked into. Instead, Desiree was made out to be a troublemaker.

During my home visits with Desiree and Ms. Grant, Ms. Grant was the first to express how she felt that Desiree was "up to no good." Ms. Grant often referred to what the behavioral specialist told her about the problems Desiree had had in her previous foster homes. It was always the same portrayal; Desiree was the instigator, and Ms. Grant was clear that this wouldn't be allowed in her home. She seemed sure that she had the answers and that Desiree would never raise her voice to her, let alone do anything else. On top of Ms. Grant's ill feelings about Desiree, when things broke at home or when anything went missing, Desiree got the blame, even though Ms. Grant also had a 17 year-old foster daughter and her 18 year-old biological daughter living within her home.

Additionally, Ms. Grant was very suspicious of me and often expressed annoyance that Desiree was involved in the program. She often accused me of taking Desiree's side, even when I expressed to her that I wouldn't take sides. She expressed on numerous occasions that she wasn't going to tolerate her name being ruined by Desiree or me. She was constantly worried that I would say something that would lead to an investigation. So for the duration of the time we worked together, she showed her resistance in different ways. If she wasn't complaining about the home visits, she was complaining about Desiree's waiver service provider Ms. Anita. However, Desiree had interviewed and selected Ms. Anita to work with her during a Meet and Greet. Ms. Anita had therefore been assigned to provide the services that were selected for Desiree from the program. Desiree was scheduled to receive skill building, family/caregiver supports and services, and planned respite. The goals that had been set for skill building included work on anger management and self-esteem, while family/caregiver supports and services was included to help build healthy communication between Desiree and Ms. Grant. Yet Ms. Grant often used the latter service to complain about how manipulative Desiree was, and how no one could believe anything that she said. She never seemed to have anything positive to say about Desiree. Instead, Ms. Grant often went on and on about how Desiree would shut down when she became upset and would refuse to communicate. While the goals set for Desiree included things like working on expressing her frustration in healthy ways along with building her self-esteem, when Desiree started to express herself she was often shut down by Ms. Grant.

Ms. Grant was aggressive and dominant. When I met with them, it seemed clear that Ms. Grant wasn't interested in letting Desiree get a word in. She also seemed to be bothered by something or someone. During a meeting in which Desiree's services were discussed, including the schedule in which she would receive her services, Ms. Grant protested about nearly everything. During this meeting my supervisor and the waiver service provider Ms. Anita were also present. Desiree's behavioral specialist participated via phone. We all observed how Ms. Grant argued about how the services would affect her schedule. However, Ms. Grant didn't have a job, nor did she even volunteer anywhere. Yet this didn't stop her from complaining about how the planned respite service would interfere with her weekend plans. Planned respite was a service that allowed the children/youth to be taken to the community to participate in positive recreational activities. Yet, while Ms. Grant expressed that having a break from caring for Desiree was what she wanted, she on the other hand continued to talk about how annoyed she was about the scheduling conflict. She stated that if Desiree was out for four to six hours for this service, she would have to arrange her schedule to be home when Desiree returned. She expressed that she didn't trust Desiree being home when she wasn't there, even when the other two teens were home. She also stated that she often had plans of her own during the weekend, and how planned respite was an inconvenience for her. We tried discussing options that included reducing the hours of planned respite, but she didn't agree to that. We also discussed having the waiver service provider Ms. Anita on occasion bring Desiree to wherever Ms. Grant was in the city to accommodate her. Yet, she continuously changed her mind about her availability and didn't hesitate to express that she felt it was all too much for her.

For several weeks she complained about the services. However, since Desiree hadn't been adopted by Ms. Grant and Ms. Grant was not Desiree's medical consenter, Ms. Grant couldn't dis-enroll Desiree from the program. So she instead turned to criticizing everything about me. She complained that I didn't seem to respect her time. According to Ms. Grant, she wanted to know at minimum a week in advance when the next home visit was scheduled for. However, I had always scheduled the home visits with her at minimum a week in advance. In fact, most of the visits had been scheduled with her and Desiree for the second visit of the month while at their home during the first visit. Out of courtesy for Ms. Grant, I also called a day before the visit to remind her that I would be coming to see them. Still, there were times when I would show up for visits and despite her knowing, she would let her phone continuously ring. On numerous occasions, there was one issue after the other with her supposedly not hearing her phone ring or the door when I rang the bell.

Nonetheless, I continued to do my job despite her many attempts to cause problems. However, when she saw that her empty complaints didn't have the desired effect, she tried even more petty attempts. She allegedly told Desiree that she didn't like me. However, I didn't get into whether or not Ms. Grant felt that way about me. I simply said to Desiree that I hoped that if Ms. Grant felt that way that she would speak with me about her feelings. However, I made sure not to focus on that issue but instead on following up on Desiree's progress or difficulties toward her program goals. When that didn't seem to work, Ms. Grant complained about me teaching Desiree how to design jewelry. I had initially started to use jewelry design as a creative way to engage Desiree during our visits. However, Desiree asked that we continue to design jewelry during future visits. As long as Desiree was able to discuss how she was doing regarding her goals, I was fine with continuing to teach her how to design jewelry. Not to mention that Desiree was good at jewelry design and she had started to feel good about what she was creating. My supervisor and the case planning team at the foster care agency were happy to see Desiree opening up and expressing her creative side. Also, there was no doubt that jewelry design was something that was helping Desiree build her self-esteem.

However, Ms. Grant expressed her frustration with this form of engagement. Even when I along my supervisor and the case planning team explained the benefits to her, Ms. Grant didn't seem to like it. In fact, during one of the visits after Desiree had designed a pair of earrings Ms. Grant did something that was strikingly odd. Ms. Grant said to Desiree, "those are nice," and asked if she could have the earrings. However, before Desiree answered Ms. Grant took the earrings and said "thanks." Things continued to proceed this way until the case planner/social worker from the foster care agency resigned. At that point Desiree's Behavioral Specialist Ms. Johnson became the go to person from the foster care agency. However, the behavioral specialist seemed to have a better relationship with Ms. Grant. They seemed to be very close, as if they had known each other for years. Perhaps it was because they shared common values about how Desiree should be raised. Ideas like the one they both expressed about Desiree's feelings of being uncomfortable, when the behavioral specialist came to visit her at school as being ridiculous. Instead of attempting to understand why Desiree felt uncomfortable, her foster mother Ms. Grant and her behavioral specialist both expressed that Desiree had no reason to feel this way. They couldn't understand how a teenage girl already struggling with her self-esteem would have a difficult time explaining to her peers why she had to have child welfare workers come to conduct school visits. Yet, they didn't offer her any guidance or support in how she could explain things. Instead they expressed that this was what was needed, and that it was just a part of her being in foster care.

Adding to their shared values, it later became even more apparent that Desiree's foster mother Ms. Grant and Ms. Johnson had the "you scratch my back, I will scratch yours" type of relationship. As long as Ms. Johnson was able to remain on Ms. Grant's good side, she could easily meet her mandated four visits per month. Desiree was required to meet with her case planner twice a month in addition to meeting with her behavioral specialist four times a month. Between the meetings that Ms. Grant had to attend with the foster care agency, in addition to the added visits from the program I worked for, maybe it became too much for her. However, because she couldn't make the decision regarding taking Desiree out of the program she continued to be as difficult as she could be. I will admit that the program I worked for had quite a number of required meetings, especially during the child's or youth's first year of enrollment in the program. So I could understand why Ms. Grant was fed up with the visits and meetings from two different agencies. However, how she went about expressing her frustration was immature and harmful to everyone involved.

It was during one of Desiree's quarterly meetings that Ms. Grant expressed that she couldn't continue to work with me. While this wasn't Ms. Grant's first attempt to show her frustration with the program, she seemed to target me. Yet, despite Ms. Grant's many past attempts to get rid of me, none of her complaints seemed valid. Her accusations and suspicions of me grew more intense as time went on. She continued to state that she felt like I would get her in trouble by reporting her to the Administration for Children Services (ACS). Yet, I continued to explain to her that I wasn't out to get her. I along with my supervisor explained my work with her and Desiree, but to little avail.

After endless accusations made by Ms. Grant during that meeting, Desiree asked if she could express her feelings about the issue. When allowed to say how she felt, Desiree had expressed that she didn't want a new health care integrator and that she enjoyed working with me. Additionally, she had explained that she was afraid to speak to Ms. Grant about certain things. Desiree expressed that she felt more comfortable speaking to me and her waiver service provider Ms. Anita. When Ms. Grant heard this she became angry and demanded that Desiree rephrase what she had said. Ms. Johnson was also bothered by this comment and quickly jumped in to state that Desiree wasn't afraid of Ms. Grant. When Desiree wanted to continue what she was saying, Ms. Johnson claimed that the battery on her phone was about to die, so she couldn't remain on the line much longer. However, she insisted that a separate meeting be held at the foster care agency to discuss Ms. Grant's concerns. I along with my supervisor agreed to participate in the proposed meeting. My supervisor asked that Desiree be present during this meeting to express her feelings about this request.

Following that meeting, my supervisor expressed to me that she was exhausted and didn't understand how I dealt with all of this during my visits. If she felt that way after one meeting with Ms. Grant, imagine how I felt after having had to meet with her twice a month for several months. My supervisor also assured me that I shouldn't worry because I had been doing great work with Desiree. However, I wasn't too worried about how things would turn out for me because I knew that I was doing beyond what I needed for my job. Plus, Desiree had been showing major improvements. Like most teens Desiree had on occasion gotten into some trouble, but it had been for things like trying to get attention by being the class clown, or for returning home an hour late after school. However, unlike most teens, instead of getting an opportunity to hang out with friends after school, Desiree had to come directly home right after the school day was over. Desiree wasn't allowed to spend time with her friends or have friends over at her foster home. Desiree continually expressed that she tried everything that she could to show that she was worthy of Ms. Grant trusting her. Yet, she still felt that no matter what she tried nothing was ever good enough for Ms. Grant.

During the time that I along with Ms. Anita worked with Desiree she had been doing her best. Desiree was showing improvements at home and at school. Despite the negative comments often expressed by her foster mother Ms. Grant, Desiree was becoming more open about her feelings and had started to use the communication skills that she had been working on with Ms. Anita. Ms. Anita had also told me that during family/caregiver supports and services Desiree was even taking the initiative to discuss household conflicts that she had with Ms. Grant or her foster sister. According to Ms. Grant, the behavioral specialist from the foster care agency had advised that Desiree and her 17 year-old foster sister avoid speaking to each other. Yet, Desiree had wanted to talk things over, especially since they shared a room with each other. However, the behavioral specialist continued to advise that they should just avoid each other. How ridiculous it was that Desiree wasn't being encouraged to discuss disagreements, but was instead told to just go on pretending that there was no tension. Nonetheless, Desiree did her best to abide by the rules and live with a foster mother who often spoke negatively of her. Desiree was very resilient and determined to do well.

During the months that I along with Ms. Anita worked with Desiree everyone noticed that Desiree seemed to be different. While she had minor disagreements with her foster sister, there had been no reports of Desiree getting into any arguments or physical altercations at school. Desiree was also able to describe positive things about herself, including that she was good at writing, designing jewelry, and drawing. Desiree had also expressed that she wanted to be a veterinarian or an actress. I at times wondered if her choice in career stemmed from her longing to have affection and unconditional love, especially given what she was experiencing at her foster home. Nonetheless, I supported Desiree in exploring her talents and was very proud of the young lady that she was becoming. I could see that she had finally started to see herself in a positive light despite the many losses and obstacles that she had faced growing up. Yet Ms. Grant seemed to have complaint after complaint regarding Desiree, the program's services, and me.

So I was a bit relieved when the day arrived for us to have the meeting that Ms. Grant had requested to discuss the change of provider. Since the program was big on freedom of choice, my supervisor and I were both supportive of having the meeting. Yet, while Ms. Grant and the behavioral specialist had agreed that Desiree would be present during this meeting, they didn't have Desiree attend. Neither of them called to inform my supervisor or me that Desiree wouldn't be present. Desiree never got the opportunity to take part in a decision that was to affect her own life. Desiree and I had developed a relationship in which she had let me in and had allowed herself to trust me despite the many times in her life that she felt she couldn't trust anyone. During the meeting everyone had agreed that since working with Ms. Anita and me Desiree had shown great improvements in her behavior within the foster home and at school. However, despite all of this including the bond that we had formed, something as petty as Ms. Grant's behavior was able to get in the way of what was best for Desiree.

On several occasions, my supervisor expressed to me during supervision that she was sure that Ms. Grant did this as a way to get closer to having Desiree dis-enrolled, or as a way of hiding what was going on within the home. Yet, even with her feeling this way, she still felt that giving Ms. Grant what she wanted was better than having Desiree dis-enrolled. However, what it really seemed like was that my supervisor was tired of dealing with Ms. Grant and was also more concerned with keeping Desiree enrolled in the program. After all, kids kept in the program meant a continued supply of billable products. It was becoming more and more evident that the goals of the agency and its stats of retained clients were more important than the well being of these children.

I met with Desiree after the decision was made, but she was very distant. How could anyone blame her; once again, a decision about her life was made by someone other than her. It started to seem like she was once again made to feel powerless in gaining a sense of control over her life. Yet, at the same time she was still obligated to meet with several providers who were all feeding to her how she would be empowered if she dealt with her past. Desiree was forced to be compliant with meeting with a temporary case planner, her behavioral specialist, with a therapist from the agency once a week, a health care integrator from the program, and a waiver service provider several times a week. So in addition to her being a middle school student and developing friends or just focusing on enjoying her adolescent years, she was often required to meet regularly with five child welfare and/or mental health providers to talk about ways to fix what was wrong with her. Yet, all Desiree seemed to want was to be with family and to be within a home that she could feel safe enough to be herself. However, that wasn't what Desiree got.

Desiree couldn't even be in touch with her biological family, unless it was during the supervised visits that she had with her brother at the residential treatment center where he lived. Her family couldn't even attend her middle school graduation. I remember Desiree expressing to me that she had asked the behavioral specialist if her biological aunt could attend her graduation but was told that it wasn't a good idea. So instead Desiree had to cope with the fact that Ms. Grant would be the only person who could attend. Imagine how hurtful this must have been for Desiree, to be forced to celebrate her graduation with a woman that she felt didn't see anything positive about her. However, the only connection that she had to her biological family is told that they can't attend.

I remember how the period leading up to her graduation was a particularly difficult time for Desiree. She had even expressed to me how much she longed that her mother were still alive. She had even said that at times, she wanted to be with her deceased mother. Yet, her feelings of sadness and loss were now being added to by the transfer of someone that she had started to feel connected to. However, just like the decision not to allow her aunt to attend her graduation or like the transfer to a new health care integrator, Desiree was starting to feel like everything was out of her hands. Shortly after the transfer took place I asked Desiree's new health care integrator how Desiree was doing and was informed that Desiree had started to cut high school. Yet, prior to this transfer Desiree had expressed to me that she enjoyed going to her new school along with the student organizations that she was interested in joining.

Additionally, the new health care integrator informed me that Desiree's waiver service provider Ms. Anita had resigned working with her due to health concerns. So not only did Desiree have to cope with working with a new health care integrator, but she also had to start working with a new waiver service provider.

Chapter Four

Just Searching for a Connection from the Past to Connect the Dots to My Present and Perhaps a Future?

Shauna

Another heart breaking experience I witnessed happened to a 13 year-old foster child who I will refer to as Shauna. Shauna's qualifying mental health diagnosis for the program was Post Traumatic Stress Disorder (PTSD) acute and Cannabis Abuse.

Like Desiree, Shauna had been in foster care for most of her life. However, Shauna had been even younger when she was originally placed within her first foster home. She had been nine months old, when she was placed in the foster home of Ms. Jenkins. According to the reports on her family history section, Shauna came into care after allegations that her biological mother had physically abused her, was severely mentally ill, and had suffered from drug abuse.

Up until the age of nine, Shauna and her three older siblings had lived with Ms. Jenkins. Up until that point, Shauna had also believed that her foster mother Ms. Jenkins was her biological mother. However, at the age of nine Shauna, her older sister Yvette, and her older brothers Michael and Mark were removed from Ms. Jenkins' home due to allegations of inadequate guardianship and failure to plan for adoption. An investigation was also called in regarding possible sexual abuse within the home of Ms. Jenkins. Following the interview with

Shauna and her siblings, along with Ms. Jenkins admitting to have tied the children up, they were removed from Ms. Jenkins' home.

Following the removal from Ms. Jenkins' home, combined Shauna and her siblings had been placed in twelve other foster homes. One of Shauna's placements included time spent at the Children's Village Crisis Residence during November 2007, following a physical altercation within one of her foster homes. In addition to her foster home placements, Shauna was also hospitalized a number of times at different hospitals throughout New York. According to Shauna's chart, her first hospitalization was at Four Winds Hospital during November of 2007 after exhibiting aggressive behavior. Shauna had also been hospitalized at South Oaks Hospital from February 12th until February 22nd of 2011 for breaking curfew and allegedly using Marijuana. However, even after I met Shauna during March of 2011 she continued to be hospitalized by the case planning team at her foster care agency. According to their reports, she had continued to be hospitalized for engaging in at-risk behaviors including missing curfew, cutting school, and alleged use of Marijuana. During this period Shauna's hospitalizations included being admitted to Stony Lodge Hospital on March 31st of 2011 and discharged on May 10th of 2011. I often thought to myself that if every teen that smoked Marijuana, broke curfew and skipped school had to be hospitalized within a psychiatric unit of a hospital, how there probably wouldn't be many teens walking the streets. Yet time after time Shauna was hospitalized for those reasons. Nonetheless, after Shauna's discharge from Stony Lodge Hospital during May of 2011 she was hospitalized once again. This time she spent a brief time at Bronx Lebanon Hospital and was later transferred to Holliswood Hospital on July 11th of 2011. She wasn't discharged from the hospital until August 2nd of that year. As disturbing as the amount of hospitalizations Shauna endured, her experiences of constantly being moved from foster homes were equally traumatic.

When I started working with Shauna during March of 2011, she had been returned to the foster home of Ms. Jenkins. It seemed odd to me that due to her other foster homes not working out Shauna would be placed back in the home with a foster parent who was once deemed to be an inadequate guardian, including having tied Shauna and her siblings up.

The first time I met with Ms. Jenkins she seemed to be fed up with Shauna. In addition to working with Shauna, I was also working with her older brother Michael. Their sister Yvette and their brother Mark hadn't been returned to the home of Ms. Jenkins following the prior removal after the ACS investigation. Yvette was eventually placed within a residential treatment facility and Mark had been placed in a different foster home. During the first meeting with Michael and Ms. Jenkins, she barely let him get a word in. She also spoke ill of both him and Shauna. Shauna hadn't returned home from school, so I didn't meet with her that day.

The first time I met with Shauna was at her school. Even though it had been our first meeting, Shauna seemed open to talking with me. It was as if we had met each other before, or as if she had been used to opening up to new workers. Sometimes it's hard to know which it is in the beginning. However, I was hopeful that it was that she felt comfortable with me. Yet regardless of how comfortable I thought she was, I didn't expect her to tell me what she did during our first meeting. The conversation had started with me introducing myself and informing her that I was the new health care integrator assigned to work with her. I had asked her about herself, and how she felt about her school. She talked about how she hated being at school, but how she enjoyed her English class. She told me of how she would at times be allowed to write songs during this class, and of her wanting to be a songwriter and rapper.

However, when we spoke of how things were going at home, including why she wasn't present the first time I came to her foster home, things took a drastic turn. Shauna's mood changed and she told me that she didn't feel comfortable being at home. Shauna had preferred to be away from Ms. Jenkins. I had thought back to my first meeting with her and how negatively Ms. Jenkins had spoken about Shauna and her brother. It didn't take much reminiscing for me to remember how uncomfortable I along with the previous health care integrator had been during that visit. We had both been relieved to leave Ms. Jenkins' home after meeting with her that day. So when Shauna had explained her feelings about not feeling like she wanted to be home, I could understand why. On the other hand, I didn't anticipate what Shauna would disclose to me next.

According to Shauna, she and Ms. Jenkins had gotten into an argument over Shauna not bringing Ms. Jenkins the type of Chinese food she claimed she had asked Shauna to pick up. The argument escalated after Shauna told Ms. Jenkins that if she didn't want the food that she would eat it. When Shauna started to eat the food, Shauna disclosed that Ms. Jenkins started to throw rice at her. They both engaged in verbal insults, which resulted in Ms. Jenkins allegedly choking Shauna. However, despite the incident that took place Shauna had claimed that she wasn't afraid to go home. It was as if this was the norm for her. It was both scary and sad that this young girl after sharing a story of being attacked seemed to express that she didn't care about returning to Ms. Jenkins' home. Even though it wasn't my job to wonder about whether or not the choking took place, I did think back to what I had read in Shauna's chart regarding her removal from Ms. Jenkins when she was nine. I mean, how could it not cross my mind when Shauna and her siblings were removed after Ms. Jenkins admitted that she had tied them up? As much as I dreaded inquiring or hearing more of this incident, I had to collect as much as I could about her physical and emotional well being. While I didn't see any bruises on Shauna's neck, I was sure that the emotional scars, though somewhat hidden, were there. As the months went by, I could see how the emotional scars manifested themselves within Shauna.

After being removed from Ms. Jenkins home Shauna was taken to a different foster home in Brooklyn. Due to the great distance to her school, Shauna was later transferred to a school closer to her new foster home. While Shauna's new foster mother seemed to really try to welcome Shauna into her home, at that point Shauna felt like she didn't fit in anywhere. Her foster mother Ms. Ray was warm, down to earth and seemed to have a loving relationship with her three other foster children. They were all biological siblings and had been with Ms. Ray for a little over five years.

However, just a week after Shauna had moved in with Ms. Ray, Shauna found her biological uncle on Facebook. After getting in touch with her uncle, he provided her with the address and telephone number of her biological mother and grandmother. Shauna shared this information with her older brother Michael who had remained with Ms. Jenkins after Shauna was removed. However, once he received news that Shauna knew where their biological mother and grandmother were, he ran away from Ms. Jenkins' home. Shauna's other older brother Mark who had been placed in a different foster home had also run away to be with Shauna, Michael, their mother and grandmother. It didn't take long after Shauna found her family that she started to return to her foster home past curfew. During one weekend Shauna in fact didn't return to Ms. Ray's home. When Shauna eventually returned, she was sent to Stony Lodge Hospital where she remained for three weeks.

During my visits with Shauna she expressed that she hated being hospitalized. She told me that she missed her siblings and that she wanted to see her mother and grandmother again. She also told me that it was strange seeing them after spending so much time not knowing who they were. However, she desperately wanted to keep in touch with them now that she had found them. When asked about how things were between her and her mother, she expressed some disappointment. She explained that her mother didn't show much interest in her or her brothers. Even though Shauna was aware that her mother was severely mentally ill and that she continued to abuse drugs, I could still see how difficult it was for her to experience what seemed like rejection. Yet even with this, Shauna told me that she still wanted to try to have a relationship with her mother. She told me that she felt a piece of her life coming together for once. However, despite Shauna's desire to maintain a relationship with her biological mother and maternal grandmother, Shauna was also aware that she was advised by the foster care agency not to see her family. It was hard to see Shauna go through this and not have any hope that she could visit her family. According to Shauna's case worker from the foster care agency, there were no plans in the works to start supervised visitation. Instead, they had plans to send Shauna to a residential treatment center (RTC). The plan was for them to keep Shauna hospitalized until a bed became available at a RTC. However, since a bed wasn't available before Shauna was discharged from the hospital, she was therefore returned to the foster home of Ms. Ray.

During the first week of returning to Ms. Ray, Shauna wasn't allowed to go anywhere without Ms. Ray. However, after that week Ms. Ray didn't accompany Shauna to school and Shauna ended up running away again. However, this time Shauna ran away and stayed with her mother, grandmother and older brothers Mark and Michael for 15 days. When the foster care agency found out about the whereabouts of

Shauna, they had her hospitalized again, this time at Bronx Lebanon Hospital. She stayed at Bronx Lebanon Hospital for one weekend and was later transferred to Holliswood Hospital where she remained for an additional two weeks. However, due to the program's policy that states that if a child/youth is missing or hospitalized for 30 consecutive days the child/youth must be dis-enrolled from the program, Shauna was now told that I couldn't continue working with her. While there are some exceptions to this, my supervisor and I had already received an exception for Shauna to remain in the program several months earlier. So we had no choice but to dis-enroll Shauna from the program.

When my supervisor and I met with Shauna for the dis-enrollment meeting, her energy was low and she spoke as if she didn't care about life. It was as if she couldn't trust anyone and didn't care where she was going to end up. For Shauna it seemed that she had been given some sense of hope when she met her mother and grandmother, but all of this was shattered when she was advised not to see them. It was hard to watch it all as it unfolded. It seemed like for a few short moments Shauna had a family, and now they were once again being taken from her life. For most of her life, she had never had the opportunity to see what her mother looked like or know whose features she had inherited. Yet, while Shauna was able to temporarily have some of the pieces of her life come together, the lack of advocacy toward Shauna's desire to be with her biological family returned her life to the broken and misplaced puzzle it had been for her growing up.

According to the case worker from the foster care agency, due to allegations of Shauna and her brothers being neglected while living with their maternal grandmother, Shauna and her siblings weren't allowed to visit their grandmother. Yet, even though her foster mother Ms. Jenkins had admitted to having tied Shauna and her siblings up, why was it ok for Shauna and her brother Michael to be returned to this foster home? It didn't make any sense to me that they could allow children to be returned to a home where a foster parent tied them up, but that they couldn't have supervised visits with their biological mother and grandmother. So I could see why Shauna was so angry about being denied the right to visit her family. Even though I didn't condone Shauna running away from Ms. Ray's home, I could certainly understand why she did it.

I later found out that for a brief time Shauna stayed at the same foster home that Desiree lived in with Ms. Grant. Nonetheless, Shauna was later sent to a group home, since a bed at a residential treatment center wasn't available. It is events like these that made me feel powerless as a social worker. When all you want to do is protect children like Desiree and Shauna, yet all you continue to see is their lives being torn to shreds, you start to feel like what you're doing is in vain. You start to wonder what is the point to all of this? It becomes hard to watch, as these children find people that they care about but have to see being pulled out of their lives. I've also wondered how I can help them feel empowered, when their lives can be changed so suddenly at the hands of someone else. I mean, is it so terrible that Shauna wanted to feel connected to her biological mother and grandmother? How heart breaking would it be for you to be separated from your siblings as a child, and when you finally find some sense of family it too is taken away from you. Unfortunately, for children like Desiree and Shauna this is their reality and they don't feel as though they have any power to change it. Some spend most of their childhood not even knowing that they have siblings.

Chapter Five

Why Do Others Get to Decide on When I Meet My Siblings?

Keyanna and Isaac

During my time working for the program, I worked with two siblings who I will refer to as Keyanna and Isaac. Keyanna's qualifying diagnosis for the program was Attention Deficit Hyperactivity Disorder (ADHD), while Isaac's was Post Traumatic Stress Disorder (PTSD). Both were African American, Keyanna was nine and her younger brother Isaac was six.

When both kids were transferred to work with me, I reviewed their charts as I always did for new clients. I noticed that they had an older sister who had been living in a different foster home, so I decided to inquire about this with their case planner from their foster care agency. I was told that none of the siblings knew that the other existed, and that in the past no one told them because they felt they were too young to know. So I asked the case planner when the foster care agency would allow their foster parents to inform them of this. I was told that their older sister was 13 and had recently been adopted. The case planner also informed me that their sister was in the process of moving out of state within the next few months. She was in fact moving from New York to Georgia.

When I met Keyanna and Isaac, they were in the process of being adopted by a couple who I will refer to as the Watsons. The Watsons were also quite concerned that no one from the foster care agency had ever told either of them that they had an older sister. However, Mrs. and Mr. Watson were advised not to bring this up due to the amount of changes that Keyanna and Isaac had gone through over the past year and a half. Both siblings had only been living with the Watsons for a year. Prior to that they had been living with an elderly foster mother who passed away. For several months the woman's daughter had tried to care for Keyanna and Isaac but due to having to care for her own young children it became too much for her to handle. So Keyanna and Isaac were removed from the foster home and went to live with the Watsons. So between the children coping with grieving the loss of their foster mother and making the transition into the new foster home, the Watsons were told not to bring up the discussion of them having a biological sister.

While everyone agreed that Keyanna and Isaac had been through difficult times, no one seemed to have any intentions or any tentative timeframe of when Keyanna and Isaac would be told that they have a biological sister. It was as if when I asked the case planner about the sister it was a non-factor. It appeared like once their sister was adopted she was no longer of any concern to the foster care agency. No one seemed to care enough to think about how any of this will affect them later on in life.

Chapter Six

Why Keyanna's and Isaac's Situation Hit Home

While I can't say that Keyanna's and Isaac's situations will end up like mine, I will say that not having a relationship with one of my biological siblings after she was adopted has done a tremendous amount of damage to our relationship. While I along with my brother went to live within a kinship foster home with our grandmother, our younger sister ended up in a non-kinship foster home.

I can remember when Tiffany was a baby and we had supervised visits with her. My grandmother and I along with my brother David met Tiffany when she was just a few months old. My grandmother had taken us to a center in the Bronx where we met Tiffany for the first time. I remember thinking that she looked like my grandmother. She had the same complexion, round face, dark eyes and a cute little nose. Yet with the joy of meeting my sister I can still remember feeling that it also felt strange to see my sister under those circumstances. There were so many strangers in that room. There was a worker from the agency, Tiffany's foster parents and of course this little baby that was my little sister. I was allowed to kiss Tiffany on the cheek and talk to her, but I couldn't hold her. Her foster parents seemed very protective of her, but I didn't know them or if she would be happy living with them.

When we left the center I asked my grandmother why Tiffany couldn't come live with us. My grandmother told me that she had asked my mother if she wanted Tiffany to live with us, but that my mother had decided not to have Tiffany stay with us. When I later asked my mother why Tiffany couldn't come live with the family, she told me that she didn't want to put too much pressure on my grandmother. She explained that she knew that my grandmother had already been taking care of my brother David and me and had also taken care of our younger deceased brother Marquis. Of course there was even more to this, when rumors started to spread around the family that the guy who had molested me was also Tiffany's father.

I remember after seeing photos of Tiffany how my Aunt Diane told me that Tiffany had resembled the daughter of the family member who had sexually abused me. So I couldn't help but wonder if this was another reason that my mother couldn't bear to have Tiffany live with my grandmother. Perhaps the thought of seeing Tiffany would serve as a constant reminder of what happened to me. Even though my mother denied this rumor having any truth to it, she also stated that she didn't know who Tiffany's father was. Despite anyone ever knowing the truth, Tiffany ended up living in a non-kinship foster home away from David and me. My brother and I only saw Tiffany a handful of times during those supervised visits.

Two years later I found out that the couple adopted Tiffany. Even though the couple had promised that they would continue visits and help Tiffany have a relationship with us, once Tiffany was adopted we no longer heard from them. As much as I wanted to see Tiffany I was told that I couldn't see her. Tiffany became almost like our deceased brother Marquis. Even though we thought of her from time to time, it was something that we were encouraged not to think about often. It was as if I had to pretend that she was gone and accept that she may never come back.

Over the years, Tiffany had only come and gone in conversations. For many years, I was left only to wonder what she was like. I wondered about a lot of different things concerning what she was like, but I mostly thought of how it would have been to have a younger sister. I thought of us playing dress up, sharing and even fighting over dolls and other toys. I thought of me doing her hair or at best trying to style it. I thought of things that I would teach her, and if we would fight over getting attention from my grandmother. Yet, for years to come that is how things stayed regarding Tiffany, limited to my childhood thoughts of what it would be like to be close to my sister.

It would end up being many years later, when I was 19, that I got the chance to spend time with Tiffany again. I along with my brother and mother met up with Tiffany in Central Park. Her foster parents had both passed away, and their adopted daughter Roxanne now had custody of Tiffany. Still, once again it all felt strange. So much had happened during those years we spent apart, so much that we didn't get to share with each other. I desperately wanted to make up for lost time, but everything was different now. We felt like strangers to Tiffany, and she felt like a stranger to us. Even though she eventually started to warm up to us, things would change.

It felt as if when the initial excitement over spending time with us wore off that the reality of the situation started to set in. She started to express her resentment about not growing up with my brother and me. At first her frustration was toward my mother for not making the decision to have her live with our grandmother. However, my brother and I eventually got grouped into her anger over not feeling part of the family for so many years. Only a few months after being introduced into our lives, Tiffany had disappeared again. Just as fast as she had come back into my life, Tiffany was gone once again. At that point I started to give up on the idea that I had a sister, and that we would ever have a bond. I hated feeling that way, but looking back, it was how I coped with the hurt of losing out on having a sister and the perceived rejection I felt when she disappeared again. Still, I knew I had a sister out there, but at the same time she seemed so emotionally distant from me. So in many ways our lack of a connection made the few times that I had seen her appear surreal, almost as if she had never truly existed.

These days when Tiffany and I occasionally speak over the phone, it's hard to see her as my sister. I oftentimes feel as though I am talking to a childhood friend I care for, but that our lives have taken us in completely different directions. Sometimes I feel guilty, as if there is something that I could have done as a kid or perhaps later on. However, I know that there was so much that was out of my hands back then. It wasn't my responsibility as a child to encourage the relationship between Tiffany and me. Instead, the foster care agency and the other adults involved should have worked to keep us in each other's life. Till this day my relationship with Tiffany is a struggle and suffers from the many years that we didn't get to build a sisterly bond. Yet, I will continue to reach out to her in hopes that in time we can have the type of relationship we both deserve with each other.

Chapter Seven

How Much Loss Can One Child Take?

Losing connections to those who should be closest to you isn't the only loss that children in foster care experience. These children deal with a number of losses and instability throughout their childhood and early adolescence that have a tremendous impact on their lives. It certainly doesn't help that workers within the child welfare system often come in and out of their lives due to the nature of the work. Sometimes it's situations like Desiree's in which foster parents don't feel like being involved with meetings and visits, so they take their frustrations out on the workers. Other times, workers and foster kids/youth part when they get dis-enrolled from programs like the one I worked for, after running away from foster homes or after being hospitalized for more than 30 days. Yet, there are other alarming reasons that some of these children experience additional loss and trauma.

Jeremy

This reminds me of a six year-old African American boy I worked with who I will refer to as Jeremy. His qualifying mental health diagnosis for the program was Mixed Expressive and Receptive Language Delay, Attention Deficit Hyperactivity Disorder (ADHD), and Disruptive Behavioral Disorder. He had been placed in foster care after being born with a positive toxicology of cocaine and alcohol. According to his chart, his biological mother wasn't compliant with her drug treatment program and consequently lost her parental rights.

When I met Jeremy, he had recently been adopted by his former foster mother of three years. He was lively and outgoing and despite his earlier childhood language delays, his verbal skills had started to improve. He enjoyed reading and was very interested in Thomas, the train toys and the cartoon show. However, according to his adoptive mother Ms. Williams, Jeremy was known to act out in school. Ms. Williams explained that Jeremy had had several outbursts over the past couple of months, but that he rarely exhibited that type of behavior at home.

When I introduced one of Jeremy's waiver service providers to him and his adoptive mother Ms. Williams, his adoptive mother shared an incident that made the hairs on the back of my neck stand up. According to Ms. Williams, two months prior Jeremy engaged in a verbal and physical outburst against his teacher after he was told that he couldn't continue to play with a specific toy. During the incident, in addition to yelling at his teacher, his behavior escalated, and he ended up kicking, biting, and punching her. So when Jeremy got home from school that day, Ms. Williams explained that in order to teach Jeremy a lesson, she did to him what he had done to his teacher. So she kicked, bit and punched Jeremy on his arm. As she told the waiver service provider and me this information, I was in shock. As the words came out of her mouth, I could see that she felt uncomfortable and surprised that she had disclosed something like that to us. I asked her if there were any other incidents like that and she stated that it was the only time she disciplined Jeremy that way. I along with the waiver service provider discussed that we would work with her to come up with appropriate ways to respond to his behavior as well as discipline Jeremy. Ms. Williams expressed that she was open to working with us to help her with coping with and responding to Jeremy's outbursts.

Nonetheless, when I returned to the office I discussed the conversation that had taken place with Ms. Williams with my supervisor. My supervisor wasn't sure if we should make a call to the State Central Registry (SCR), but stated that she would discuss this with her supervisor, the Bronx program director of the program at our agency. After my supervisor had a discussion with the program director we were told that since the incidents occurred before our agency was involved, and since Ms. Williams had understood that what she did was wrong, there was no reason to make a call to the SCR. Instead, I was advised to keep my eyes open for any other incidents or any strange behavior. I felt uncomfortable being in this situation, but being new to the agency I didn't want to challenge the program director or my supervisor's recommendations. While I couldn't shake what Ms. Williams had told me, for the next two months I did as I was advised. However, things continued to happen over the next couple of months that started to make me question if I had made the right decision.

At first, it was an incident following an agency picnic held for the children and their caregivers which Jeremy and his adoptive mother had attended. A few days after the picnic I noticed that Jeremy had a scratch on the side of his head. So I asked Jeremy what had happened. However, before Jeremy could answer Ms. Williams interjected and began explaining that it was an accident that had occurred at the program's picnic. According to Ms. Williams, she was trying to remove Jeremy's shirt so he could use the restroom and her nail accidentally scratched him. Her story seemed a little odd, but I didn't want it to appear that I was conducting an investigation. After all, it wasn't my job to investigate abuse. Besides, if I had to make any calls later, I wasn't sure if I necessarily wanted Ms. Williams to know that I was the one who made the call. I was very aware of how uncomfortable things can get after calls of this nature were made. So I continued with our visit as if I accepted her account of the incident. Yet, once again I got a weird feeling about the incident that I couldn't shake off. My feelings about how deep the scratch looked compared to how she explained how the scratch had happened started to give me a strange feeling in my gut.

Once again I had to share what I had witnessed with my supervisor, but once again my supervisor stated that accidents like this are very possible. However, since I hadn't visited Jeremy's school at that point, my supervisor agreed that it would be a good idea to speak with his school counselor and/or his teacher. So I informed Ms. Williams that I would be conducting a school visit, and she didn't seem to have any concerns regarding this.

When I visited Jeremy's school, I was able to meet with the school social worker that Jeremy met with once a week. The social worker explained some of the behavioral difficulties that Jeremy had displayed in class over the past two months, including the incident that Ms.

Williams had discussed in which Jeremy had physically attacked his teacher. The social worker also explained that when Jeremy attended school the day after the incident had taken place, she noticed that he had a scratch on his forehead. The social worker had written a letter to Ms. Williams inquiring about the scratch. However, according to the school social worker, Ms. Williams appeared very defensive within an email that she sent responding to the social worker's inquiry. The social worker stated that she had on occasion asked Jeremy how Ms. Williams responded to him after that incident but that Jeremy wouldn't talk about it. When asked to show her how he was disciplined at home, Jeremy had always been hesitant. However, there was one occasion that Jeremy demonstrated and tried explaining to the social worker that Ms. Williams made him stand in a corner when he got in trouble. When the social worker brought this topic up at different times, she explained to me that Jeremy would get quiet or would change the subject whenever she inquired about how Ms. Williams treated him after he got in trouble at school or at home. The social worker expressed to me that her gut feeling was telling her that something wasn't quite right, but that she too didn't make any calls to the SCR. Jeremy's school social worker then asked if I wanted to have Jeremy's teacher join us. I agreed in hopes that she would have additional information about Jeremy's behavior in class. His teacher explained that his behavior was getting better, but that from time to time he had a difficult time with sharing with his classmates. However, instead of being aggressive towards his classmates, Jeremy would instead become aggressive toward her or other staff. Jeremy's teacher also explained an incident that had occurred around a month prior in which Jeremy was misbehaving at school, and Ms. Williams showed up at his school. According to his teacher, when Jeremy saw Ms. Williams enter his classroom, he immediately started to cry.

After meeting with Jeremy's teacher and school social worker, the uneasy feeling I had when Ms. Williams first disclosed how she disciplined Jeremy came back to me. Yet, once again I was told by my supervisor that if something was going on, the school social worker or the teacher would have called the State Central Registry (SCR). It was as if no one wanted to be responsible for the call but everyone had the same feeling.

The last straw was during another home visit in which Ms. Williams told me that Jeremy had been moving his bowels on himself within the last week, coupled with me seeing that Jeremy's knees had been scratched up. According to Ms. Williams, Jeremy had fallen at the playground. However, this time when I got to the office, I expressed to my supervisor that I no longer felt comfortable not making the call to the SCR. My supervisor agreed, and we made the call. However, things became even more strange when the operator at the SCR explained that she wasn't sure if the call would be escalated to warrant an investigation. Even after we explained to her the other incidents including the scratches, the accounts from Jeremy's school social worker and teacher, not to mention Ms. Williams openly admitting to kicking, biting and punching Jeremy just a few months earlier, she was uncertain about an investigation being opened. So the operator explained that she had to get her supervisor to join in on the call. The supervisor decided to accept the call and explained that an investigation would begin.

Although there was a sense of relief that someone would be investigating, I was also very concerned about how Ms. Williams would react. Rightly so, because Ms. Williams called my supervisor and explained that she no longer wanted Jeremy to participate in the program. Since she had adopted Jeremy, she was now his medical consenter and therefore could legally make the decision to dis-enroll him from the program. This was very concerning because since Jeremy had been adopted there were no longer visits from social workers from the foster care agency. So when she dis-enrolled him, the only social worker in his life would be the school social worker who hadn't previously followed through with her suspicions of abuse.

Ms. Williams ultimately got what she wanted and dis-enrolled Jeremy from the program; however, not before explaining to my supervisor that when she met with the child protective specialist from the Administration of Children Services (ACS) the worker had stated that she didn't understand why a call was made. According to Ms. Williams, the worker had expressed to her that she had bitten her child one day to teach her a similar lesson. When my supervisor shared this with me I was baffled. I was just as confused as I was when the operator expressed uncertainty about whether or not to accept the call. While on one hand it was hard to believe that a person sent from the ACS would actually conduct herself in that manner, let alone share this with a parent that she was investigating for physical abuse of a child, on the other hand I had seen equally bizarre findings from a written report from an ACS investigation with a different client. So even though the information was hearsay, I wasn't sure what to believe.

Chapter Eight

The Nightmare Being an Elderly Foster Parent Can Become

Like Shauna who had been dis-enrolled from the program due to being hospitalized for 30 consecutive days, there are other children who share a similar fate. While it is disturbing to have a child hospitalized for 30 consecutive days, I have witnessed that it is equally challenging for a grandmother caring for her granddaughter to experience this.

Cassie

Cassie was an 11 year-old African American girl who had lived with her maternal grandmother Ms. Carrington from the time she was born. Both Cassie and her 16 year-old sister Christina had lived with their grandmother due to their biological mother's psychiatric history and inability to care for Cassie and her older sister. Cassie had been enrolled in the program during 2010 to help her with managing her aggressive behavior, including her verbal and physical outbursts towards her grandmother. Additionally, Ms. Carrington was to receive support in coping with and responding to Cassie's mental health needs. Cassie's qualifying diagnosis for the program included attention Deficit Hyperactivity Disorder (ADHD) and Oppositional Deviant Disorder (ODD).

During 2009 Cassie had become physically aggressive to the point that her grandmother asked the foster care agency to temporarily remove Cassie from her care. As Ms. Carrington had requested, Cassie was sent to a therapeutic foster boarding home during September of 2009 with Ms. Garrison. It was said that Cassie did well within the home of Ms. Garrison and that her behavior began to improve. Therefore, it was decided that Cassie could be returned to her grandmother's home on a trial discharge during July of that year.

However, when Cassie returned to her grandmother's home she had also returned to the type of behavior that had once resulted in her being removed. When asked to do chores, or when told that she wasn't allowed to go somewhere or to have something that she wanted, Cassie lashed out at her grandmother. Nevertheless, Ms. Carrington was very protective of Cassie and feared that if Cassie got removed again that it would show that she couldn't care for her. So Ms. Carrington did everything in her power to show that she was willing to be the type of caregiver that Cassie needed. Not only did she cover for Cassie when Cassie became abusive towards her, but she participated in every program that was recommended in order to have Cassie remain in her care. This of course included attending parenting classes required to maintain custody of Cassie, along with attending family therapy, and eventually her participation with the program I worked for.

Having Cassie enrolled in the program meant that Ms. Carrington had to be open to the home visits with Cassie's health care integrator (HCI) and waiver service provider (WSP). Cassie's grandmother also had to participate with Cassie and her WSP during family/caregiver supports and services. However, it didn't stop there because Cassie's 69 year-old grandmother also participated in the program's required meetings like the preliminary meeting, initial meeting, two quarterly meetings, and the reauthorization meeting. Along with those required meetings, Ms. Carrington was also responsible for taking Cassie to her weekly individual therapy appointments, monthly medication management appointments with Cassie's psychiatrist, to Cassie's medical appointments, meetings at the foster care agency, and of course, parent-teacher conferences at Cassie's school. All of this for a 69 turning 70-year old woman who had undergone knee surgery and walked with a cane. Yet, Ms. Carrington was very determined to take care of Cassie and her sister in order to keep their family together. So it was heartbreaking to see how things unfolded for them after Cassie was hospitalized during April of 2011.

According to the waiver service provider, Ms. Carrington had informed her that Cassie had engaged in aggressive behavior towards her grandmother, which included punching and biting Ms. Carrington after an argument. The incident had resulted from Cassie being told that she had to return a video that she had borrowed from the library and her refusal to do it. Cassie's waiver service provider provided crisis respite and took Cassie out into the community to separate Cassie from her grandmother. The waiver service provider temporarily removed Cassie in order to give her some space and time to process what had occurred. However, during the time that the WSP took Cassie out of her grandmother's apartment, things took a turn for the worse. When Cassie demanded that the WSP purchase a toy for her and was told by the WSP that she couldn't purchase the toy, Cassie engaged in an outburst. According to the WSP, Cassie began to yell and run away from the WSP on their way back home. The WSP was able to catch up to Cassie but the WSP had become very fearful of how dangerous this could have been for Cassie if she had run into the street and was hit by a car.

Upon returning to Ms. Carrington's home the WSP called 911 and Cassie was taken to the emergency room at Bronx Lebanon Hospital on April 2nd of 2011. On April 4th Cassie was hospitalized within the inpatient psychiatric unit for children and adolescents. However, Cassie hadn't been a stranger to being hospitalized as she had stayed at Four Winds Hospital from July 10th of 2009 until September 15th of that year. Yet, regardless of her prior experience of being hospitalized Cassie continued to express that she didn't want to remain in the hospital.

Cassie pleaded to be returned to her grandmother's home and professed how she would behave differently if she could go home. However, this time things were different. Ms. Higgins, the hospital social worker assigned within the children and adolescent psychiatric unit at Bronx Lebanon Hospital had coincidentally worked with Cassie and her grandmother in the past. In fact, Ms. Higgins had worked with them when Cassie participated in a similar program prior to her 2009 hospitalization at Four Winds Hospital. According to Ms. Higgins, Cassie had actually engaged in similar types of behaviors and had also run away from a waiver service provider and into the streets during a planned respite session.

Additionally, Ms. Higgins had reported that when Cassie stayed within the foster home of Ms. Garrison after the 2009 incident, she had seen Cassie at her best. Ms. Higgins also stated that there was more structure and appropriate discipline at Ms. Garrison's home. So Ms. Higgins was very concerned about whether or not having Cassie return to her grandmother's care was in the best interest of Cassie or her grandmother.

However, during the times that I met with Cassie and her grandmother, they had both been very adamant about having Cassie return to her grandmother's home. However, this wouldn't be the case this time around. Additionally, there were no other relatives who could care for Cassie. Her mother who suffered from schizophrenia and was living at a home for severely mentally ill adults had already had her legal guardian rights taken away. The only other relative that Cassie had known of was her uncle who according to Ms. Carrington used illegal drugs. So between the concerns expressed by the hospital social worker Ms. Higgins, the concerns by the other mental health professionals working with Cassie and her grandmother, and the fact that there were no other viable relatives to care for Cassie, the foster care agency expressed that they felt it would be best to have Cassie sent to a Therapeutic Foster Boarding Home (TFBH) following her discharge from the hospital.

After being informed of the hospital staff and the foster care agency's sentiments, Ms. Carrington was distraught but reluctantly agreed to have Cassie sent to a different foster home. Still, her anger didn't go unnoticed. After all, she had done everything she was asked to do, from the meetings required by the hospital to the program's meetings including a reauthorization meeting to continue services for the upcoming year, to a preservation placement conference coordinated by the foster care agency. Despite her age and how exhausted she was, she had also managed to visit Cassie in the hospital every day. So hearing that Cassie wouldn't be returning to her home was devastating. She expressed to me that she felt defeated and like nothing that she did mattered. However, she was clear in expressing that she would continue to fight for Cassie.

Equally hurt by the news that she wasn't going back home after leaving the hospital was Cassie. I noticed a complete change in how open she was with me. Perhaps in her eyes she felt that anything she said would somehow be used against her and would prevent her from ever returning to her grandmother's home. So Cassie went from openly discussing her feelings to being closed off and answering questions with short answers if anything at all. Since Cassie had once enjoyed drawing and coloring during our meetings, she had asked if she could keep the paper and crayons at the hospital and use them after our meeting. Even though she continued to draw and color during our meetings, our conversations were kept to a minimum and she remained withdrawn. I couldn't help but to think of what it must have felt like for her to be worried about saying something that would hurt her or her grandmother. Despite the difficulties in their relationship Cassie had always expressed that she loved her grandmother. Likewise her grandmother had expressed and showed that she cared for Cassie a great deal. Yet, despite their love for each other neither of them knew what their futures would hold, specifically where Cassie would call home. Cassie's social worker from the foster care agency informed me that the foster home that Cassie had lived in during 2009 wasn't an option due to the number of children currently living with Ms. Garrison. So this meant that Cassie would have to be sent to a different foster home.

After two weeks of searching for a foster home, the agency had identified a potential foster parent and informed Cassie and her grandmother. However, the foster mother ended up changing her mind, and Cassie and her grandmother were once again left wondering where Cassie would go after being discharged from the hospital. At the same time, the deadline for the extension to continue Cassie's program services was getting close to expiring, and none of us knew when Cassie would be discharged from the hospital. My supervisor and I had advocated for Cassie not to lose services, but my supervisor had been informed that if by the time we attended the preservation placement conference the foster care agency hadn't identified a new foster home, we would have to dis-enroll Cassie from the program. The only way that we could have avoided doing this was if we had been provided with Cassie's discharge date by one of the hospital's staff that had been working with Cassie during this time. However, according to Ms. Higgins, the hospital social worker, Cassie wouldn't be discharged until a foster home was ready for her to be sent to. Still, it had been over a month that Cassie had been hospitalized when the preservation placement conference took place at the hospital. Yet, the social worker from the foster care agency had explained that they were still waiting for a foster home to become available.

It became clear during the meeting that my supervisor and I would be meeting with Ms. Carrington and Cassie to hold the dis-enrollment meeting. However, before we even got to that point there had already been so many different emotions expressed, so I mentally tried to prepare myself for what could transpire during the dis-enrollment meeting. Like Cassie who had become withdrawn, and frustrated by how things were turning out, her grandmother had also expressed those sentiments. In particular, Ms. Carrington expressed her annoyance about the continued meetings that she felt she had to participate in, none of which she felt could help bring Cassie back home. During the preservation placement conference, Ms. Carrington even shouted out as tears ran down her face that she didn't understand why we continued to have her come to all of those meetings when we would do what we wanted to do anyway. As she cried, I thought of Ms. Carrington being my grandmother and how I hated seeing this elderly woman appear so defeated and powerless, especially while Cassie stood there watching all of this unfold. Yet, I also felt a bit defeated, and despite wanting things to have turned out differently I realized that Cassie wouldn't be going back home to live with her grandmother after leaving the hospital. There was a major part of me that wondered between Ms. Carrington's age and her health concerns if Cassie would ever return to her care.

Chapter Nine

How Many Times Does One Need to Cry Out Before Something Is Done?

Cari

Like Jeremy, Cari, a 15 year-old African American adolescent, had also been in foster care and had therefore had an ACS investigation conducted. Cari's qualifying mental health diagnosis for the program was Adjustment Disorder with Mixed Disturbances of Mood and Conduct. However, prior to being enrolled in the program during 2009 Cari had entered the child welfare system based on circumstances involving her mother's struggle to care for her. When Cari was ten years old she had been removed from her mother's care due to allegations of inadequate guardianship, specifically her mother's use of illegal drugs and abuse of alcohol. According to Cari's chart, on June 4th of 2005 her mother Ms. Mead and her mother's boyfriend Craig abused alcohol in front of Cari until they became intoxicated. Ms. Mead and her boyfriend Craig also engaged in a physical altercation in front of Cari, which included objects being thrown around the apartment and near Cari. It was reported that Craig pushed Cari, which resulted in Cari's mother stabbing Craig's hand. Cari witnessed the entire incident, but thankfully didn't sustain any physical injuries.

Following Cari's removal from her mother, Ms. Mead checked herself into a 28-day detox at an inpatient substance abuse facility. However, at the time Ms. Mead's case worker had recommended that

Ms. Mead seek treatment at a 6-12 month inpatient detox facility. However, Ms. Mead was concerned that she might lose her apartment and consequently didn't follow the case worker's recommendation. Instead Ms. Mead ended up staying at the 28-day detox for 24 days due to altercations she had with other patients. The child protective specialist who had investigated the June 4th allegations referred Ms. Mead to an outpatient substance abuse facility. While Ms. Mead attended the intake appointment, she missed the follow-up appointment. Ms. Mead was also referred to a family preservation program, but wasn't compliant with the required home visits and meetings. When asked why she wasn't compliant, it was noted that she expressed that she was "hanging out" and "had things to do." The child protective specialist scheduled an elevated risk conference during August of 2005 to discuss Ms. Mead's plans to comply with the requirements needed to regain custody of Cari. While Ms. Mead was aware of the meeting, she didn't attend. Following Ms. Mead's non-compliance Cari was sent to live with her biological father. At this time Ms. Mead once again checked herself into an inpatient substance abuse facility during October of 2005 but left against medical advice the following month.

While Cari temporarily stayed with her father during 2005, she ended up running away and returning to her mother's apartment. When it was discovered that Cari had returned to Ms. Mead's home she was taken away and placed with her maternal grandmother. However, once again Cari ran away from this kinship foster home and returned to her mother's apartment. Due to Cari constantly running away she was sent to a higher level of care at the Pleasantville Cottage School during January of 2006. Cari remained at the school until she was trial discharged to her mother on June 26th of 2009. However, on November 9th of that year the trial discharge with Ms. Mead ended due to a physical altercation between Cari and her mother. Consequently, Cari was placed in a non-kinship foster home with Ms. Washington. According to the reports, Ms. Washington stated that Cari did well within her home, including keeping curfew and doing chores. However, in February of 2010 Cari was returned to the care of her mother Ms. Mead.

Yet when I met Cari and Ms. Mead, it was clear that they were both crying for help. However, perhaps due to frustration based on their history of non-compliance, it seemed like I was the only one fighting to help them make changes. When I began working with Cari during March of 2011, she was still on trial discharge with her mother Ms. Mead. As much as I wanted to support Cari remaining in the home of Ms. Mead, all signs were pointing that this wasn't a good idea. After just a few visits with Cari and her mother, I had seen a young girl desperately looking for stability, structure and, of course, unconditional love from her mother. However, due to Ms. Mead's continued drug and alcohol abuse she couldn't provide Cari with the kind of care and home Cari desperately needed.

Yet, the case planner and her supervisor at the foster care agency seemed to have the kind of attitude that they had washed their hands of this family. I remembered those actions or lack of actions from Shauna's case worker. Perhaps it comes from hearing about struggles from other workers who have worked with the client(s), or perhaps from their own battles with the client(s). Still, regardless of how frustrated we become, I deeply feel that it is up to us workers to acknowledge the signs of getting to that point and to understand how it is affecting our working relationship with a client. However, this level of understanding seemed to be missing from this particular case planning team. The workers were instead hard to get in touch with and no longer seemed to put this family and their needs on the forefront. The case planner and her supervisor expressed that they felt powerless to do anything because Ms. Mead had continuously missed meetings and often evaded the scheduled home visits. They also expressed that it was useless to have Cari go to another foster home because she had previously run away from each foster home and back to her mother. I read in Cari's chart that she had temporarily stayed with her older sister up-state New York. However, when Cari's sister refused to send Cari back to the Bronx to see their mother on their mother's birthday, Ms. Mead told her oldest daughter to have Cari return home for good. Yet, Cari's chart had also stated that Cari responded quite well when she lived with her older sister, including doing well at school.

On the other hand, back in the city and at Ms. Mead's apartment Cari continued to go downhill. Not only was Cari constantly cutting school, breaking curfew, and hanging out with the wrong crowd. Over the past year she had also been arrested three times. Each arrest progressively got worse. Her first arrest was for train surfing, her second for vandalism, and her third for assault and attempted robbery. Cari seemed to be crying for help, but no one from the foster care agency seemed to be interested in doing anything about it. Instead, it was like they were looking to push Cari off to a different set of workers. Sometimes my supervisor and I actually discussed how it appeared that they were looking for someone else to take care of what they perceived as the problem family. Maybe they were tired of trying, or perhaps they were fearful of the risks associated with having such a high-risk family. It often came across that the case planning team was eager to keep Cari enrolled in the program that I worked for in order to show a judge that Cari was receiving sufficient community support and could therefore be ready for a final dis-charge to her mother. After all, once children/youth are final discharged, the foster care agency is no longer involved. When children are final discharged, the health care integrator/social worker is responsible for taking on the role previously held by the case planner from the foster care agency. So along with the duties required from the program, the HCI would also be responsible for making any referrals including support with housing, entitlements like Medicaid, or other community referrals.

However, it was clear to see that things were getting worse with Cari, and that her home wasn't providing the kind of stability and structure she needed in order to do well. Plus, Cari's waiver service provider whom she had previously been connected to and had started to open up to had recently resigned due to personal obligations. A major concern was that Cari had made it clear that she wasn't open to any new waiver service providers. She had stated that if a new waiver service provider were assigned to work with her, she wouldn't participate in any of the services. At that point she had become fed up with new workers coming in and leaving.

It became increasingly difficult to get Cari to speak, and when she did, she stated that she didn't want to live with her mother. I explained to Cari that I wasn't in charge of whom she would live with and encouraged her to speak with the case planner at the foster care agency. However, she expressed that they never did anything. Likewise when I spoke to Ms. Mead, she expressed the same sentiments that the foster care agency wasn't doing anything. She even told me that she had told them that she was actively using crack, and that they didn't even make a call to ACS. She stated that "this is crazy," and indeed it was. She proceeded to yell and state that she was "tired of all of this" and that she wanted to get Cari out of the program because it wasn't helping her. She expressed that Cari no longer wanted to be involved and that it was a waste of time. I informed Ms. Mead that I would speak to my supervisor and schedule a meeting to discuss Cari being dis-enrolled from the program. Ms. Mead said that she would be available for the meeting.

When I returned to the office the following day, I informed my supervisor of this, and she explained that she would discuss it with her supervisor. Of course, after hearing that Ms. Mead was interested in dis-enrolling Cari from the program, things seemed to be more urgent. Yet, my previous attempts to get everyone involved to see how desperately this family needed more support seemed to get little response. It was like pulling teeth to get anyone motivated to act, but when a parent threatened to take away a source of income from the program this somehow warranted immediate action. Of course, this also got the attention of the case planning team from the foster care agency. Without the program, it would make it harder to present to any judge that Cari was ready to be final discharged to her mother. I mean, considering the fact that Cari had been arrested three times in one year, had been cutting school, not coming home on time and had a mother who was admitting to actively using crack, how could any reasonable judge final discharge Cari to her mother? So a meeting was in order.

However, due to the case planner and her supervisor not being available for the dis-enrollment meeting on this day, just my supervisor and I went to meet Ms. Mead at her home that Monday morning. When we arrived I buzzed the intercom, but no one answered the buzzer. So we waited for several minutes, and after ten minutes I rang the buzzer again. There was still no answer, so I called Ms. Mead's mobile phone. To my surprise she answered, but stated that Cari wasn't home. I told Ms. Mead that my supervisor was with me, and that we were there for the dis-enrollment meeting to sign Cari out of the program. Ms. Mead said that she was heading downstairs to open the door.

When Ms. Mead came downstairs, she seemed erratic and stated that she was going to the store to get a beer. She told my supervisor and me to go upstairs and that the door to her apartment was open. She also yelled out as she was walking off, that my supervisor should get her notebook out and get ready to write. I could see that my supervisor was very uncomfortable, but we nonetheless went upstairs and waited for Ms. Mead to return. When Ms. Mead came back from the store, she placed her beer on the table and proceeded to enter her bedroom. She was yelling and telling someone to put on their clothes and get out because she needed to meet with us. A few minutes later a man left the bedroom and exited the apartment. My supervisor became increasingly uncomfortable as the man left and Ms. Mead continued yelling. Ms. Mead stated that she was getting high and that this wasn't a place for Cari to be. Ms. Mead also stated that she hadn't seen her daughter since Friday morning. She reported that she believed that Cari may have been with her friend Keisha, but stated that she wasn't sure. The entire time she paced back and forth throughout the living room and was drinking her beer. My supervisor asked her if she was able to discuss Cari being dis-enrolled from the program, and she yelled out that she no longer wanted to be bothered. She stated that she didn't need to have a meeting but was willing to sign the loss of eligibility form to dis-enroll Cari from the program. Even though Ms. Mead signed the form provided by my supervisor, she also wrote on it "Fuck You." So needless to say, due to Ms. Mead's being high and intoxicated we weren't able to accept her signature to dis-enroll Cari.

Following the meeting, we headed back to the office and immediately informed the case planning team from the foster care agency of what had occurred. We also had to call the State Central Registry to report what we had witnessed and been told regarding Ms. Mead's use of drugs and alcohol along with her not knowing where Cari had been over the weekend. The call was accepted, and an investigation found that Cari needed to be removed from her mother's home. Cari was therefore placed within a foster home. Yet, after staying for one night Cari returned to her mother's apartment. Her mother expressed that she wouldn't deny Cari and would always welcome Cari back into her home. So the foster care agency decided to call a meeting at their office to discuss the recent events and plans for Cari's placement. Since the earlier dis-enrollment meeting didn't take place, the case planning team agreed to have both meetings on that day.

Before the meeting took place the case planner emailed me an attachment with the findings that ACS had made from a prior investigation. According to the report, the findings stated that even though Ms. Mead had admitted to actively using crack cocaine, there had been no evidence that she had done so in front of Cari. The investigation was therefore closed, and Cari was able to remain with Ms. Mead at that time. I couldn't believe that in writing I saw a document that basically stated that a mother could keep custody of her child, even though she had openly admitted to using illegal drugs. Not to mention that she was caring for an adolescent who was engaging in at-risk behaviors including being arrested three times in one year. I wondered what the outcome would be from this investigation, if the previous one basically allowed Ms. Mead to continue caring for Cari just because there was no evidence that she was using drugs in front of her.

Nonetheless, my supervisor and I attended the meeting held at the foster care agency's office. I was pleasantly surprised to see Ms. Mead attend and to see her sober. Ms. Mead had also expressed that she didn't want Cari to remain in the current foster home, but instead that she wanted Cari to move to California to live with Cari's sister-in-law. Cari was informed by the case planning team and a representative on behalf of her law guardian that this process wouldn't happen over the next week or two. Ms. Mead asked if in the meantime the case planner could look into a substance abuse treatment facility that would allow her and Cari to live together while Ms. Mead received treatment. While the case planner wasn't aware of a program like this, she stated that she would look into it. However, the case planner's supervisor encouraged Cari to remain in her foster home and to abide by the rules in order to help support the possible short-term plan at the treatment center and the long-term plan to move to California with her sister-in-law. Although Cari was reluctant, she agreed to remaining in her current foster home and to attending school to show that she would do well in California. In addition to this, Ms. Mead proceeded to sign Cari out of the program and signed the necessary documentation dis-enrolling Cari from the program.

Chapter Ten

Through the Belly of the Beast: Life Experiences and My Path to Social Work

For many years I wanted to separate my experience of being in foster care from my career choice. I hated the idea that I would become a social worker just because I had lived certain experiences. I also didn't want to have the attitude that surviving my traumatic childhood meant that I was an expert. I understood even before I made the decision to be a social worker that each person is unique including how we experience the world around us. However, to say that my life experiences didn't shape my decision to have a career in social work would be naïve. Growing up in foster care definitely had an impact on my choice to work in foster care.

Until you're in foster care it's hard to know what it's like to be taken away from your parent(s). But try even for a moment to consider being a child, more specifically think back to being seven years old. The world is still new to you, unfamiliar and enormous. However, your family is supposed to provide a sense of security, safety, and love. In particular your mom, dad, grandparent(s) or whoever your caregivers are in a lot of ways are the glue that holds your world together during this period. Regardless of whether your parents fight with each other, yell at you, or hit you, you still see them as your protector. In your eyes, they may even represent some type of God-like figures. Now imagine being a seven year-old kid and being told that workers from ACS are coming to take you away.

I remember feeling hunted down by the ACS workers because my mother often evaded them. On numerous occasions, ACS workers would come to the homes of my mother's family and friends looking for my brother and me. Every time the workers came looking for us, family or my mother's friends would lie and say that my brother and I weren't within their home. Once someone called my mother and told her that they were threatening to arrest her if she didn't bring us in or call to have us picked up. Following that news, my mother agreed to have us taken from her care.

When my mother finally decided to have ACS workers come to get us, she explained to me that David and I would be picked up from our grandmother's apartment. I can remember the look on her face when she told me. Her dark eyes were filled with fear and were on the brink of releasing tears. Yet, my mother even in that moment of uncertainty and utter sadness held back from showing how defeated she felt. Even though I was afraid, I wanted to protect her. I wanted to tell her that things would be alright, even though I had no clue of what would happen. Instead, she hugged me for a brief moment and told me that she loved me. The unexpected hug from my mother who had always had a difficult time expressing her emotions was very comforting. Still, other than knowing that I was being taken away from my family, I didn't know what to expect from that point on. When she saw how terrified I was, she told me that my grandmother would end up getting us to live with her. While I wanted to believe her, my mother had been inconsistent and unpredictable. So it was hard to know if she was telling me what she thought I wanted to hear or if there was any truth to her words. So I was left to wonder about how things would unfold over the next few days. Wondering about how things would turn out unleashed something inside of me. Until that point those emotions had been tightly packed away for years, while I tried to escape the reality of my twisted childhood.

So that night I cried alone in my aunt Diane's apartment. I hated crying in front of my mother because she always seemed so sorry for the circumstances that we were in. My mother also seemed childlike in my eyes and appeared to be very vulnerable. As a child I was always afraid for her safety, as if she could be easily broken. So the night my mother told me that my brother and I would be taken away from her, I hid my tears from her and everyone else. That would be the beginning of many years of hiding my tears and isolating myself during my most difficult times. That night I cried soft enough not to be heard, yet deep enough for my fears to surface. It was as if my tears had fallen so hard and so deep that they had awakened everything inside of me. All of my insecurities, every wonder of how my now uncertain future would be and every fear of loneliness that I sensed were all alive from my tears. Part of me wanted to stop crying because I feared getting caught by mother. However, my mother had left my aunt's apartment to have another hit of crack, perhaps in an attempt to erase the conversation that we had just had. Her leaving gave me permission to cry, and I found myself no longer having to hold back the tears that were begging to be released. Once they started to flow down my face, I no longer wanted to hide them. Yet, still I thought to myself how my mother hated when I showed weakness. Crying to my mother was a sign of giving in. Yet, over the years I have come to see that my tears showed her the truth behind my forced smiles. Perhaps seeing how truly hurt I was in those moments triggered her guilt, especially during those moments when she was sober. Yet, that night I didn't have to worry about her seeing my tears as an act of weakness, or my enormous sadness. That night she was off into the night to hide in her own weakness and vast sadness. I barely slept that night, and the following morning she returned to take my brother and me to our grandmother's apartment. We took the number 2 train from 135th to 110th Street, and not much was said during that ride.

When we arrived at my grandmother's home, a few family members were there. My grandmother, my cousins Patrick and Asia, and an uncle we all called Jr. were there. Each family member spoke to me and reminded me of how much they loved me, and that grandma would fight to get us back. My grandmother told me not to worry and that as soon as she could go to court she would. My cousin Patrick who had often teased me was so sweet that day. He bought me a candy necklace and comforted me. All of their love made it even harder when the doorbell rang and the workers from ACS arrived.

It felt like in just a matter of minutes all of the people that I loved and that loved me were being taken from my life. I looked around and the adults who were supposed to protect me were all crying and appeared helpless. No one told me where I would end up or who I would live with because they didn't know. I wasn't even aware of how long I would be away or if I could ever return to visit my family. There was definitely a part of me that sensed that my world was about to forever be changed, and it definitely had.

After we left my grandmother's home, my brother and I were taken to an unfamiliar place and surrounded by child welfare workers asking me what seemed like pointless questions. Then I remember waiting, and waiting and just waiting, only to be shuffled off to a van. One of the child welfare workers told me that they had found a new home for me. The worker seemed relieved to tell me the news. It was as if in her eyes a new home and a new life would solve all of my problems. Better yet, she described her finding a new home for me as if it were a prize. A prize that had the promise of being everything I ever wanted. But it wasn't a prize and I didn't feel as if I were gaining anything. I instead felt like I was losing everything that mattered to me. I remember thinking to myself that this wasn't what I deserved. I hadn't done anything terrible to deserve what my life had become, and yet I couldn't do anything about it. I was just a kid in a world that I felt I had no control over. However, regardless of what I felt, at that point I knew that I was going to live with someone other than my family. Even at the age of seven, I could understand that it was a new way of being, with new people. At that age, this experience and my expectations of my future were incredibly unfamiliar and scary.

I remember asking the worker if my brother would stay with me and being told that he would. However, when it was time for him to be dropped off at his foster home, I was told to stay in the van. Suddenly the cold reality hit me; the worker had lied to me, and it became even clearer to me that I couldn't be certain of anything anymore. I cried but it didn't do anything to change what was happening, because there was nothing that I could do. I was just a helpless kid with people that didn't know me making decisions about my life. All of a sudden everything was changing and it was like I was expected to just deal with it. I was expected to fit into my new home and my new life and just accept that this was the way things would be. I felt powerless. I felt just like the once God-like figures that I saw weeping and powerless to stop my brother and me from being taken away. As if being taken from the last thread of my family wasn't enough, I had to get through the night in a new place that I was told would be my home. I remember being shown to my room since it was so late, and being told that I would share it with her other foster child. There were bunk beds in the room and it seemed girlie and clean, but it wasn't my home. When my foster mother said "welcome home," I put on a forced smile. My smile was full of resentment for the words that she uttered. "Welcome home, welcome home," they played in my head like a stupid yet catchy song that you can't shut out, or like the death of someone you can't ever forget.

Once again, I had a sleepless night as I lay on the bottom bunk bed. I thought of what my mother said about it being temporary, but I also thought of how she often lied when she thought it would protect me. I also thought of the case worker who had lied and said that my brother would be placed with me. So as I lay down on that bed I felt terrified and desperately alone.

The next morning my foster mother introduced me to her other foster daughter. It was just like that, there was an expectation that I no longer had a brother or a large family, and now I was supposed to just adjust to my new life. My foster mother told me that she would take me shopping soon, but in the meantime that I could share the clothing of her daughter. As excited as I used to get about clothing, not even that could shake me out of what felt like an awful dream. Part of me felt like maybe this is my new reality and that I should try to find the positive side. So I thought of how my foster sister appeared to be polite and generous to me there. Maybe it was because she was told to behave this way, or perhaps she wanted someone close to her age to spend time with. Either way, she offered to share her toys and overall seemed happy to have me. I was also polite and expressed my appreciation, but slightly expressed my desire to return to my life at home.

I remember telling her what my grandmother had told me about going back home. However, she didn't seem to believe it, or maybe since I barely knew what to believe, I wasn't all that convincing. As I spoke about my family I desperately wanted to go home. I worried about my baby brother David and if he felt safe or scared. I wondered if he looked out for a familiar face and if he cried when one wasn't present. I wondered how they responded to him, and if they were patient with him, or if they yelled at him when he cried. I started to hate myself for not being able to protect him and everyone else for not keeping us together. More and more anger grew inside of me, and I wondered how my mother and family could allow us be taken away. Yet, I also remembered their vulnerability and uncertainty as we were escorted out of my grandmother's home. I also remembered what my life had been like before the fateful day that the ACS workers came to remove us from our mother's care.

Before that day, I had spent several years moving from one place to another. My mother often frequented the homes of different friends or acquaintances while getting high. Before my brother David was born I was dragged along with my mother to accompany her to get her fix. We went to several places where drugs were sold and plenty of places that drugs were smoked, shot up and/or snorted. I saw crack bottles, needles, pipes, cigar filling and people whom I considered the walking dead. While my mother went into a room to smoke, she would see if I could watch TV or see if she could purchase me a cheap toy to keep me occupied. Sometimes one or two of her drug buddies would come out and start speaking with me. When she would hear them talking to me, she would rush out to come check on me. When she returned from smoking, her behavior was often strange. She was paranoid and often asked me to check her skin. She always thought that something was crawling on her. I would constantly have to assure her that she was fine and that there were no bugs on her. When she started to come down from her high, she would be incredibly apologetic. She always needed me to say that I wasn't mad at her. So I had no choice but to keep telling her that I wasn't mad at her. Eventually, my anger became sadness for who she was becoming. I suppose it was also a bit a sorrow for who I was becoming.

When I lived with my mother from birth until the age of seven, I missed several days of school. I was often in jeopardy of being held back. Thankfully I was somehow able to have teachers who would give me the extra help that I needed in order to get promoted to the next grade. However, missing school wasn't without consequences. In fact when I was six, I along with a group of two other students spent our first grade year in a kindergarten class. It was a way for us to get things that we had missed, but we were also taught some lessons separately with just our group. However, both the first graders and the kindergarten class teased us because we were neither. We were stuck somewhere in the middle.

Titania at Age 5

I remember that even at that age my peers had created a normal and a not-so-normal group. Being part of the not-so-normal group meant that I was on the outside, and being on the outside made me feel different. Feeling different wasn't what I was aiming for, especially at that age. The feeling of not being like my peers highlighted my feelings of loneliness and self-doubt. It made me feel that I wasn't good enough, or like I had done something terribly wrong to deserve how my life was at that time. Those feelings of insecurity struck me at my very core and started to eat away at how I viewed myself. I started to see who I was as wrong, bad, and not worthy. After all, I had also come second to my mother's addiction to drugs and the men she chose to feed her addiction. Having my peers torment me about things that were out of my control also made me feel powerless. This feeling would continue with me for many years and affect every aspect of my life. After all, I couldn't force my mother to take me to school. Most of the time she was exhausted or I was from our constant moving around. I can remember how she would ask me if I wanted to go to school. How could she ask me such a question? I mean, how many kids would choose school over sleeping in late, playing with toys, and watching TV? Not to mention going to a place that I didn't fit in. At the age of six, I definitely wasn't equipped to make decisions about my education. However, on many occasions she would leave the decision up to me, and on many occasions I would choose to stay with her. Perhaps on some level I was also anxious of not seeing her when I returned from school. Plus, back then I was exhausted from worrying about a number of things. Anything from my concern about her safety to what crazy situation she would have us in that night. So there was always an ample amount of things to be anxious about, and adding school to the mix wasn't of interest to me.

Each experience had its own level of fear and concerns that came along with the situation. In particular, I remember being on high alert when we went to strange apartments. Although the people varied somewhat from place to place, each of those places had a certain emptiness about them. It wasn't just the emptiness of the people that filled the apartments, but I can remember that visually they were often dark and lifeless places. Even on the brightest afternoons those apartments were dark. It's as if the darkness on some level hid the truth about what they were doing. They were perhaps comforted by the darkness of those rooms. But the darkness didn't comfort me. The absence of light terrified me. I couldn't see where my mother went, and I couldn't see what she was doing. Yet perhaps in some way the darkness acted as a shield for me. Maybe not seeing what she was doing protected me from the visual of my mother's enemy. Back then I wanted to leave, but I couldn't leave her in those dirty and dingy places. Some of those apartments were the most filthy places I had ever seen.

One place in particular I remember so clearly because till this day the sight of cigarette buds or used matches on a floor makes me sick. I associate those things with filth and my memories of that one apartment I despise. My mother had an acquaintance by the name of Bill. Even though she hated coming to visit him, the supply of drugs was too alluring to ignore. He lived in a studio apartment in Harlem. It drove me crazy that the brownstone he lived in was so beautiful and well kept, yet his place was a disaster zone. Dirty dishes lay everywhere and clothing thrown every which way throughout his dingy apartment. Yet most of all, used matches and cigarette buds covered his floor. I hated entering his apartment and remember feeling angry towards my mother for making me go there. My mother could tell from the look on my face that I was uncomfortable. She often laughed as she pointed out my obvious uneasiness of being in his home. I would sit on his bed and make sure that my feet, even with my sneakers wouldn't touch his floor. My mother would often laugh and comment on what she would say was a certain look I gave. She would say, "stop acting like that when we go to his place." At times she would have to remind me to stop while we were in his home. I remember one time Bill even laughed and said to her, "stop bothering her, I know it's bad." I thought to myself that walking on the street felt cleaner than the floor of his apartment. She had the nerve to make it seem like I was the one at fault. She was embarrassed by my behavior, when Bill should have been embarrassed for keeping his home so filthy. Or how about her, she should have felt bad about having me stay in a place that made me sick to my stomach.

Yet once again I had no choice, my mother's addiction had overtaken my comfort. Her addiction often took over her ability to consider my comfort and safety. Unfortunately for me, my concerns went beyond nasty apartments. My apprehensions even extended beyond the times that my mother had disappeared into those bedrooms or bathrooms to use drugs. On those occasions she had accompanied people who like her had filled themselves with substances that seemed to numb their reality. They had even become numb to the people that truly mattered. So numb that they appeared empty, just like I had perceived those apartments.

However, the apartments had been full, full of people coming in and out, and full of enemy substances that eroded their lives. I also became full, full of anxiety over my mother's safety and at times my own. Yet mostly, I was afraid for my mother. I knew what she was like when we were together, and the risks that she took. I can remember the arguments with men that were double her size and that no doubt towered over me. I also knew that my mother was bold, reckless and seemed to do whatever she felt was needed to score her next hit. My mother was full of scams to get her way. On several occasions during the late hours of the night, she and I would take cabs even though she had no money. She would wait until we arrived and then tell the cab driver that she didn't have any money. Sometimes they would threaten to call the cops, other times they would threaten to drive us back. Sometimes she would tell them that she could get the money from her friend. She would even leave me in the cab while she went to ring the doorbell. She later told me that at times she intentionally rang the wrong doorbell in hopes that the cab driver would believe her attempt to pay for the ride. Either way, it was frightening hearing these men yell and threaten my mother. Not to mention that it was scary being left in the backseat of cabs with drivers that could have taken me anywhere. So with my mother making decisions like that with me, needless to say when she left me behind, I feared for her life.

However, there were times when it seemed like she put more thought into my brother's and my safety. I can remember one of her friends by the name of Scott. Scott lived in the basement of a brownstone on the same block as her acquaintance Bill. The brownstone was nice, but the basement was creepy. Scott was a tall, dark skinned, bald and elderly man. Scott had grown up in the South, and you could still hear his southern accent. Scott was definitely our protector and did what he could to look after my brother and me when my mother left us behind. So on many occasions Scott ended up watching my brother and me while my mother ran the streets. He seemed to genuinely care about us, and I could see by the look on his face that he was worried when my mother stayed out late. He especially seemed to be bothered when she stayed out later than she had said she would.

There was one occasion when my mother stayed out particularly late but had promised me that she would return with White Castle burgers. I waited for her and didn't eat the food that Scott had made for dinner earlier. I was so sure that my mother would return with dinner. I was so hungry and afraid that I started to wonder if something violent had happened to her. Finally, I convinced Scott to call my grandmother. Scott didn't have a phone in his apartment and had said that he didn't have any money to use a pay phone. I urged him to make a collect call to my grandmother. My grandmother was horrified and sent my grandfather to pick my brother and me up. Even after my grandparents had fed us, I was still worried about my mother. The next day when my mother returned to Scott's apartment, she realized that we were with her parents.

At the time that was my life. Filled with fear and anxiety over my inconsistent and my ever-changing world. At that age friends were also hard to keep. Not only did I rarely stay in one spot, but inviting my friends over wasn't something that was possible. Most parents wanted to know that their children would be in a safe environment. Yet, I had no one place to call my own and of course couldn't guarantee a safe place to invite my friends over to. Living with Scott, despite how much he protected us, felt too strange to explain to my peers. Needless to say, during those years making and keeping friends was hard. However, while it was hard thinking of ways to explain my circumstances, there were some kids that made it more comfortable. Perhaps I sensed that they too had circumstances similar to my own, or maybe we bonded based on proximity.

In fact, Kim comes to mind when I think of those days. Kim was actually the only friend I had when I lived on that block. I had met Kim while living with Scott because her mother shared the lower level of the brownstone. Kim's mother was a thin-framed and petite woman. June was her name, and she was every bit as pleasant as her name. Looking back, I feel that June felt sorry for me because she could see how isolated I was. She could clearly see that my mother was heavily addicted to drugs. There weren't many secrets you could keep on that block. So seeing me day after day left alone probably pulled at her heart because she often tried to include me in activities with her and

Kim. However, most of the time, my mother was hesitant about me spending too much time with them. Back then I couldn't understand why my mother would deny me a friend, but now I see that she tried as much as possible to keep our secrets safe. The less other people saw, the less likely it was that other people would interfere.

Yet on the occasions that she allowed me to hang out with Kim, I would mostly spend time playing with Kim's toys. Kim had every toy imaginable, including a huge collection of Barbie dolls. On one hand I envied Kim. I mean, Kim seemed to have it all. She not only had every toy that I wanted, but she had a safe home, with a loving and dependable mother. June seemed to cater to Kim's every want and need. June appeared to put Kim first, while my mother seemed to put everything and everyone before my most basic needs. On the other hand, Kim was deaf, and even back then I could see how frustrating it was for both of them. Sometimes my mother would tell me that she felt bad for Kim because she could see that June at times pushed her too much. My mother used to say that June pushed Kim to try to communicate what she wanted, and that June always had a let-down look when Kim couldn't express clear enough what she wanted. My mother even went as far as to say that June wanted me to spend time with them because secretly June wanted me to be her daughter. Back then I believed nearly everything my mother said. Perhaps there was some truth in my mother's perception, but I also believe that her words came from her own insecurities. Either way, I treasured the times that I spent with Kim and June. Being with Kim helped to ease my loneliness. Despite Kim not verbally communicating with me, we kept each other happy. Perhaps we were friends because we both had experienced what it was like to feel different, or perhaps it was based on us happening to be neighbors. However, either way my relationship with Kim and June was comforting and helped me to have healthy connections. Besides, it seemed like if Kim wasn't with her mother, she was alone. So I am sure that our relationship worked both ways. However, even keeping Kim as a friend was difficult with my mother constantly moving around. From the age of five and a half until age seven Kim and I were friends. However, after I was taken from my mother, Kim and I lost touch with each other.

Losing touch with friends became something that I grew to deal with, but it was also something that deeply bothered me. In many ways it felt like I was robbed of healthy bonds with peers, especially outside of school. I wanted so much to feel like everyone else and hang out at my friends' homes or have them hang out at my home. Yet I didn't have a home, and my lifestyle of always being on the go made it impossible for me to feel connected or safe to form lasting friendships. Instead, I often kept to myself and learned how to be my own best friend. I created a separate world that no one could enter. I mostly built my own world because I felt so different from everyone else, but also because I was afraid of losing friends when the inevitable move would take place. The many inconsistencies of my life and the secrets I had to keep held me back from getting too close to other kids, even at school. Even though I was able to meet new people and at times carry on some sort of friendships in school, over the years they didn't feel deep or particularly meaningful. Everything felt on the surface, as I shared only what I was willing to risk. After all, my life had already been full of risks that my mother took and plenty of uncertainty from her actions. Like the many friendships that came and went over those years, it was also hard to keep things like my favorite toys or drawings, or other crafts that I made for my mother in school.

During the years leading up to me entering foster care I had stayed in endless shelters with my mother. It was always the same. We had to spend nearly an entire day or at times stayed overnight downtown at the Prevention Assistance and Temporary Housing (PATH) office, waiting to be placed in a shelter. There were crowds of people waiting just like us to find a temporary place to live. Once a vacancy in a shelter was found, a van would take us to a shelter. One of my first memories of living in a shelter was being in a large room with beds lined up beside each other and lockers along the walls. I also remember not having any privacy. Sleeping in a room filled with strangers and strange sounds made it hard to sleep. I often only fell asleep after the exhaustion of running around and from the many new things that I faced each day. Keeping my possessions was another issue during this time. When my mother would bring my toys to the shelters, they were either stolen or left behind when my mother would leave the shelters for more than a night. This would happen time and time again as my mother failed to follow the curfew of the shelters. So anywhere my mother went I had to go, and whatever was left behind became up for grabs. Even though she tried to make it feel like an adventure, even as a child I knew what was going on. I knew what I had been losing and missing out on, but I kept my mouth shut and wore a smile to comfort my mother.

So even though I hated the idea of my brother and me being taken away from my mother and our other family members, I could understand how the life we lived with her wasn't the way that children should live. Still, even with my understanding, I wanted to be back with my family. As traumatizing as the removal was for me, fortunately my brother and I only stayed in our non-kinship foster homes for a weekend. We had been dropped off late one Friday night and were taken to family court the following Monday.

In family court, a social worker asked how I felt about living with my grandparents. I explained to her how badly I wanted to live with them and of course how much I had also missed being around my other family members. Right after answering her question I asked if I could see my brother. After a series of questions she took me to see him. David and I were in a play area while we awaited our fate. I was told that my grandmother was speaking with the judge. It seemed like we waited an entire lifetime before a decision was made. However, when I finally saw my grandmother's face, she wore a smile. She said that the judge said that we could live with her. With a warm smile on her face she spoke the words that I had longed for, we were coming home.

Grandma Mary

Grandpa Aaron

My Grandparents Together

Chapter Eleven

Back Home to My Grandparents

My grandmother and grandfather's home was always the place that everyone had gravitated to. That apartment was lively with family members sleeping everywhere from bunk beds, to pull-out beds, to people sleeping on the couches and even the floors. Holidays and birthday parties always included a lot of people, food, drinks and the occasional blow up if someone had too much to drink. There was plenty of laughter, especially when my cousins Patrick and David and my uncle Jr. started telling jokes. I loved it when the adults used to play a card game called Spades and I used to sit close to the table as I watched and learned. As I grew a bit older I would sometimes get to play a hand of Spades, but Spades was mostly what the adults played when everyone got together. Us kids were happy to just have one of those ten cents frozen ices, or one of those 15 cents firecracker icy pops while we watched them play.

At times it felt like the entire family stayed at my grandparents' home, perhaps because at one point or another we all did. But that's the way my grandparents were, always willing to look out and keep the family together. They had both been born and raised in the South and moved to New York City as young adults. My grandmother had come from Columbia, South Carolina, and my grandfather from Charleston, South Carolina. My grandmother's name was Mary Bly, and she had gotten the last name after marrying my grandfather Aaron Bly. However, when my grandmother gave birth to my mother, she still had the last name of her previous husband. Hence, my mother's last name being Grace and mine being the same. Nonetheless, not even something like a different last name changed how things were between my grandpa and me. My memories of grandpa were mixed mainly because he appeared to be as scarce around the home as my mother had described he was during her childhood. However, grandpa had been in the U.S. Navy during a great portion my mother's early childhood.

Grandpa was light skinned with curly dark brown and gray hair. Growing up, my mother had told me how much of a ladies' man he was known to be and of the rumors that often spread around the neighborhood of his extramarital affairs. Yet, she had also told me that while she believed the rumors, my grandpa tried his best to keep things concealed out of respect for my grandma. However, as a child I wasn't aware of his relationships outside of the home, but I was greatly aware of his gambling and constant need to be out. I remember coming into the place where he used to play his numbers, and how anxious he was to see if he hit any numbers. I also remember how he used to sing a song before we ate dinner that went something like, "Eat your Food and Eat it Fast, if You Don't, I'm Gonna Beat that Ass." As young kids we used to find his song so hilarious and crack up at the table. However, later on I remember my grandmother giving him a look that meant "cut that out," and how his version of the song was later cut off at the tail end where he used to say "Beat that Ass."

My grandpa was an interesting character and spoke in a fast and matter of fact kind of way. His speech was comical and he was definitely a straight shooter when he told stories. Grandpa wasn't afraid to tell you like it was or how he saw things to be. However, sometimes he was honest to a fault like the time I overheard him yelling at my grandmother telling her to give me the money for the tooth fairy. She had originally asked him to leave some money, but he instead said, "Why don't you leave the money for her?" As a kid I rarely ever believed in things like Santa or the Tooth Fairy, mainly because my mother made it clear to me early on that they weren't real. I suppose she got that from her father, along with the difficulty to show her emotions. My grandpa definitely came across as tough.

However, even with his tough exterior I knew that my grandpa loved me. Grandpa showed his love in ways like when we spent quality time together, while he watched and verbally critiqued the news. It was funny to see him because he became so passionate about world politics that he would speak as if he were having a debate with someone. My mother used to tell me that as a child she used to get so embarrassed when she had friends over because they would ask, "Who is he speaking to?" She would jokingly reply that he was just talking to the TV. However, I found it sweet that he would let me sit on the bed watching him while he sat on his recliner by the window wrapped up in various debates. He also showed his warm side when I used to have nightmares and needed to sleep in the middle of him and my grandma. He was understanding, even when I wet the bed. So even though he spent most of his time outside of the home, when he was at home it was clear that he cared about me.

It was also clear that my grandpa and grandma had very different personalities. My grandma was very warm, inviting and seemed to be the type that was born to be a mother. Her love, like her overall essence was vast. While I often envied how much I had to share her with my cousins, I always knew that she loved me. I also loved her dark complexion and how she kept her mostly gray hair braided. We often joked about her braids because they were so matted from her wearing her wigs that you could barely see the actual braids when she took her wigs off. She was very often simple in appearance except for her floral-printed, summer-like day dresses that she wore to do everyday household things.

My grandma was such a great cook and could always find a way to turn anything into something that tasted like it came from a five star restaurant. Like her sardines and rice that, even though they smelled like something I wouldn't touch let alone eat, I somehow devoured. I loved the way she made cabbage and, of course, how she made collard greens like nobody's business. Her fried chicken and baked macaroni and cheese tasted like heaven. She even got me into eating pig feet and chitlins, a stew of pig intestines. As gross as that may sound, preparing them smelled even worse. As I grew older, I used to help her clean and cut up the chitlins. While I detested the smell, when my grandmother was done preparing it, I couldn't believe my taste buds. Those chitlins were so tasty, especially with hot sauce.

When she made Sunday breakfast, the whole apartment was filled with smells of pancakes, sausages or bacon, or at times sliced ham slightly fried. Even when she did something simple, like make grits with eggs and corned beef hash, she knew how to throw down. When she made anything, it somehow turned out to be the best meal I had ever eaten. Just like her cooking skills, her baking was like nothing I had ever eaten. She prepared everything from cornbread to cakes, including her upside down pineapple cake and, of course, her sweet potato pies. Her sweet potato pies had just enough sugar, vanilla extract, nutmeg, and cinnamon. I will always miss how she made banana pudding or a summer time treat she prepared with strawberries, sugar and Cool Whip. Sometimes I would get a chance to help her butter and flour the pans when she baked cakes or cornbread. As a treat she would let us kids have the remainder of the cake mix left in the bowl. I loved finishing the cake mix and would take my fingers to get the last bit of it off the bowl.

Like her cooking she put everything into caring for her family. Every cousin, aunt, uncle and even family friends loved my grandmother. My grandmother held the family together, and her home was a safe haven for my cousins who were in similar situations. Specifically for those of her grandchildren whose moms could no longer care for them. So my brother and I joined them in the three-bedroom apartment, the same apartment we often frequented when my mother had dropped us off in the past.

When my brother and I moved in with our grandparents, it was bittersweet. On one hand we had a home with our family, on the other our mother was still roaming the streets and heavily addicted to drugs. While we had gained a sense of stability, my constant fear of where my mother would end up continued to be on my mind. I so badly wanted my fears to go away. Yet, I couldn't shake my concern for her safety. I often thought of the erratic and dangerous things she used to do for money and wondered what it would be like, now that I wasn't around to protect her. When we were together people would feel sorry for us, but I could imagine that people weren't as compassionate when she was alone. All sorts of things would go through my head, like would she trick another cab driver and be taken off somewhere and get killed? Would she promise a guy she was getting high with something and then go back on her word, making the guy furious? Perhaps the guy would be so high from drugs that he wouldn't even realize what he was doing. Would anyone even know where she was heading when she left? Were any of those people even sober enough to remember?

I can remember as a child living in the same building with a girl close to my age who was murdered over drugs. The girl's mother had gotten into an argument over drugs that were promised to a guy she was dating, and he threatened to throw her daughter out of a window of the high-rise building she lived in. When the argument escalated and he didn't get the drugs that he was promised, he threw her daughter out of the window. This actually happened in the same high-rise building in which my grandmother had lived. Prior to her addiction to crack/cocaine, my mother used to work as a home health aide for an elderly woman within the building. According to my mother, while working, she heard a loud thump come from outside. She figured that it was someone throwing trash bags out the window, but when she heard people screaming she realized it was something more serious. When my mother went downstairs, she saw the little girl dead on the floor.

After the incident, Jasmine's mother always had a vacant look on her face. When my mother and I would see her in the building or around the neighborhood, my mother would always say how sad the entire situation was. As a kid hearing about what happened to Jasmine made me even more worried about things like that happening to my mother. Even though I was just a child, I often saw myself as my mother's protector. When my grandmother would get upset with her for not spending time with my brother and me, I would try to defend my mother. When case workers told me that my mother would never get custody of my brother and me, I defended her. When my mother stole clothing, sneakers, and even underwear from my cousins and they wanted to beat her up, I physically got in the middle.

There was one incident in particular that actually terrified me and caused me to try and physically stop one of my older cousins from beating my mother. I begged for my grandmother to help and break up the fight, but she stood there and said that my mother had to learn. I didn't care about my mother learning some lesson about stealing clothing in that manner, I just didn't want to see her get hurt. While on drugs, my mother had become very thin and was an easy target. So I had to jump in and try to pull my cousin away from her. It was awful on so many levels, but it particularly bothered me that the three of us prior to that had such a close relationship. My cousin's name was the first name that I was able to clearly speak. I used to want to spend every second with her and her friends. In many ways she was my older sister, and I had looked up to her. Yet, in that moment my trust for her had forever changed. I had a decision to make, and my loyalty had to be with my mother. So I fought for my mother's survival. I was just a kid and couldn't do much, but I was happy that I stood up for my mother and disappointed that my grandmother in that moment didn't. Till this day, as much as I love my grandmother, part of me always holds some resentment for her letting them fight over stolen objects. Objects that could and were easily replaced. Yet, I have to live with that memory for the rest of my life. So despite living in one home, being inside of my grandmother's home was also uncertain and made me fearful of what my future would hold. Besides, after that altercation had taken place in the apartment, in addition to me having to worry about my mother's safety while she was in the streets, I now had to worry about her safety at home. I often thought to myself that we both seemed so weak in a world that seemed so tough. I had doubts about how we would survive it all. So with a place to consistently lay my head at night, my mind was often roaming in the streets where my mother had roamed.

There were certain things that, even though my grandmother tried to protect me from, she felt powerless to prevent. Although my grandmother appeared to do her best under the circumstances to ease my fear of how things would turn out, it had been obvious that my grandmother couldn't completely take away my anxiety. Yet, my grandmother would hold me in her arms and tell me that everything would be ok someday. She would tell me not to worry because she was there and that someday it would hurt less. I later found out from family discussions that my grandmother had also experienced being abandoned by her mother at an early age. So she knew what it felt like not to have a nurturing mother who was fully present. She understood the feelings of emptiness and self-doubt because of her loss. It often felt like my grandmother and I shared a bond based on our mutual pain. At the time I was so young that I couldn't clearly see how hurt she must have been. Not only did my grandmother have to cope with her mother not being around, but she also had to raise her younger siblings. Yet my grandmother was good in concealing her pain from us grandchildren. Her pain became masked by our pain.

My grandmother's life was one of tragedy, but also of great strength. Even after a painful adolescence of loss and forced responsibility, during her adult life she had nine children that she cared for. Her entire life was spent caring for others, including the many grandchildren that were either adopted by her or came in as foster kids. Not to mention the amount of grandchildren that unofficially ended up staying with her from different points, when their parents weren't healthy enough to care for them. It all took a toll, but my grandmother continued to do her best to provide us with a loving home. She even tried to encourage our parents to visit and spend time with us within her home.

However, when my mother came to visit, most of the time was spent recouping from her nights of using drugs. So she often came to the apartment exhausted, dirty, and hungry. So I had a few moments of quality time with her before she crashed and a few moments before she headed back out to use. Back then I was just grateful to spend any time with her and to know that she was safe. Eventually, my grandmother started to get annoyed that my mother and her sisters were using her home to rest, shower, and get food. So my grandmother tried to push them to take us out when they came to visit. While my grandmother had the best intentions, the same couldn't be said for someone with a sickness that obscured his morality. All of the best intentions in the world couldn't stop his intentions with me.

Since I used to accompany my mother to several homes while she was addicted to drugs, I became an easy target. It was only a matter of time before I became tangled up in the lifestyle that we lived at the time. Even though I had been to many of the crack spots I had been fortunate to avoid any major trouble until one afternoon. As I had feared, my luck ran out one day and my life would forever be changed by the course of events that took place in one of these homes.

Darren was a relative through marriage and his apartment had been one of the places I accompanied my mother to on a number of occasions. Darren had also lived on the same block as Scott and Bill, so before I moved in with my grandmother his place was one that my mother and I frequented. However, being in his home always gave me an eerie feeling. I later found out that there was a valid reason for my gut instincts. There had been rumors around the family that Darren had paid people to engage in sexual acts with him. It had also been said that he engaged in these acts with family members. Yet, I soon realized that Darren's sexual desires went beyond his desire to be with adults. This all became crystal clear when he started to molest me. However, before Darren started molesting me, I remember being in his studio apartment where he molested one of my family members. On a few occasions, I saw him and two of my family members go behind the curtain that divided his living room area from the kitchen and bathroom. At the time I had been behind that curtain only to use the restroom, so I couldn't understand what they were doing behind it. I just knew that when my family members returned to the living room how different one of them looked. When she had come out from the curtain, she always had a distant look on her face, and her mother seemed focused on heading towards the door. I suppose he grew tired of being with my relative because he later chose me.

I was five years old when it all started. However, instead of going behind the curtain that I had seen my relative go behind, things unfolded on his pullout couch. In his apartment I experienced things that no child should ever have to go through. He engaged in sexual acts with me, including performing oral sex on me. He even attempted to have intercourse me with on several occasions, but never fully went through with it. Each time he molested me, I am sure he could see how confused and uncomfortable I was. Still, nothing seemed to matter to him but feeding his sexual perversion.

In an attempt to prevent me from telling anyone, Darren used money, toys, and fear to manipulate me into silence. He bought my first roller skates and my first bike. How awful to have my memories of what should have been joyful moments destroyed by him. The sexual abuse and the secret continued without any disruption until rumors started to spread within the family. When my grandmother questioned me about the allegations, I cried. I cried out of pain, and out of fear for what this meant. Yet, there was also a sense of relief that came over me as I thought of how I no longer had to keep it all to myself. My grandmother also had a way about her that comforted people, especially during times like this. So I told my grandmother everything that had happened, as I sat on her bed. As the words left my mouth, I could see how angry and hurt my grandmother was. Still, as comforting as my grandmother was, I was very concerned about how the events would unfold after I broke my silence about the sexual abuse.

However, Darren was never reported. While I never got the truth behind him not being reported, it was later said by a relative that no one reported him out of fear that I along with my cousins could be removed from my grandparent's home. On top of him not being reported, the sexual abuse continued on and off until I was ten years old. While my grandmother had suspected it, and at times had asked me, I couldn't bring myself to tell her what was going on. I had thought to myself that nothing seemed to happen to Darren, yet how it had been emotionally draining for me to discuss what was going on. So I concealed the sexual abuse to avoid talking about it and out of fear of being taken away. So I dealt with the abuse until I became mature enough to understand that I was being used and manipulated. I remember feeling angry and hurt that my relative was allowing this to happen. I eventually told the relative that had been allowing the sexual abuse that I would tell my grandmother the truth if she ever brought me back to his place. Even though the sexual abuse stopped at that point, there was a period that I did my best to try and forget about those days and nights I had spent with Darren. I instead tried to focus on being a kid and losing myself within the love I could get from my family.

Chapter Twelve

At Times a Blessing

While there was no denying that my grandmother had a full home, there were also times that living with such a big family provided the comfort and laughter that helped me to deal with the hard times of my childhood. We often looked out for each other, and having a big family in the neighborhood often meant that bullies rarely messed with me. If one of them did, one of my cousins would be right there to find out who it was and was ready to stand up for me. They also made sure that I knew how to defend myself, but the intimidation of our family was often enough to keep most bullies away.

There were other times that I look back to and laugh about. I think back to when us girls got our hair straightened in the kitchen, while my grandmother used the stove to heat up the straightening comb. Of course, I can't forget how my grandmother would always say, "hold your head down" or "keep your head straight," when I used to jump from the sound of the hair grease sizzling from the heat of the comb. But I loved the look and feel of my hair after she was done, so I endured the sizzling sounds of the hot comb while I thought of how I would swing my hair back and forth. Or when I started to wear beads at the end of my braids with the foil wrapped around the ends to keep the beads in place. I loved swinging my braids. I definitely enjoyed wearing my hair in beads more than having my hair in tight ponytails with those colorful barrettes in my hair. Other than those times, I along with Latoya, whom we all called Toya, used to wrap a towel around our heads and pretend that it was long flowing hair. Remembering times like that definitely makes me laugh.

Or times like when my cousin Patrick used to do what we called "snap" on me, which meant telling jokes at my expense. Back then snapping on people was a big deal, and the better the joke or comeback, the bigger the laughs and bragging rights you would get in the neighborhood. My older cousins Patrick, David, and McClinton, whom we called Mack-a-do, along with my uncle Jr. and my second cousins Stevie and Gregory were the best at snapping. For some reason, I was terrible at snapping and the only laughs I would get would be from how corny something I said had sounded. Like snapping, we did other silly things in that apartment that kept us entertained. One of my favorite games was blind man bluff where one person who was tagged wore a blindfold and had to go around a dark room chasing everyone until someone else was tagged. We used everything from bandanas to scarves to shirts to tie over the person's eyes. I couldn't help but scream when the person who was tagged got close to me. I would often give myself or the person next to me away. I remember one time that my cousins got so pissed off that they told me that I couldn't continue playing with them. When my grandmother saw me crying in the living room, she asked what happened. When she found out that they kicked me out of the room, she told my cousins that if everyone couldn't play that no one could. So when I went back in the room my cousin Asia said "forget it," and they ended the game. Even things like that make me laugh, when I look back.

I also miss the times, when we watched movies in the living room as a family, even the scary ones like *Nightmare on Elm Street* and *Friday the 13*th. The living room became the main area for entertainment within my grandparent's home. This also meant that the video game systems were placed in the living room, including the *Nintendo* system where we all enjoyed playing *Mario Brothers* and the *Sega Genesis* where I loved playing *Sonic the Hedgehog*. Having one TV with cable that was placed in the living room at times was a bit annoying. It obviously meant that we all had to share and at times watch shows that we didn't want to see. Nonetheless, it also meant that I got a chance to watch a bit of everything. For the most part I enjoyed watching the shows that my cousins wanted to watch. I remember watching everything from *The Care Bears, The Smurfs, Punky Brewster, Mr. Rogers, Tom and Jerry, Duck Tales, Alvin and the Chipmunks*, to *The Simpsons, In Living Color, Full House, Family Matters, A Different World* and *The Fresh Prince of*

Bel-Air. I was even allowed to watch movies like Spike Lee's *School Daze* and *Jungle Fever* and of course the R&B and rap videos showed on Video Music Box. Regardless of what I got to watch and/or wasn't supposed to see, when I think about the time spent together with my family I always miss those days we sat in that living room watching TV. Or times like when Mary and I used my easy Bake Oven to the point that Mary got sick from eating strawberry-flavored cake. Till this day Mary won't eat any strawberry-flavored cake. I also think of Mary's mother, who was always lively, full of laughter and always started the party. She had insisted that all of the nieces and nephews call her Aunt Pat. She was so well loved and respected that all of us always referred to her as Aunt Pat. Plus, if we didn't she wouldn't respond to us until we called to her how she expected us to. Aunt Pat was not only fun during parties, but she was also cool to hang with on any other occasion. Like when she used to take us kids for free lunch at local schools during the summer and had us laughing at her jokes or just her larger than life personality.

Like Aunt Pat, my Aunt Sharon was also fun to hang with. Sharon often reminded me of my grandmother's youngest sister, Aunt Evelyn. Both had a very gentle and generous personality and were fun to be around. I remember how Sharon used to have tea parties with me, or how she would tell me that if I helped her with the laundry she would buy me some goodies. Since my grandmother would at times help her out with some extra cash for doing our laundry, Sharon figured that she would have some company while she did it. However, her asking me to help really meant that she just wanted someone to chat with while she did the laundry. Although as a kid, I really thought I was being a big help and at times I did help fold. Nonetheless, my true motivation at the time was the reward of getting to buy more snacks with the 50 cents she gave me. Thinking of those moments reminds me of how sweet and nurturing she was.

When my Aunt Sandra, my godmother came around, she was also sweet, as she would listen to me go on and on about how I loved to sing and dance. Aunt Sandra was the type of person who, even though I was a kid, listened to what I had to say and made me feel like what I said really mattered. I loved how fast she spoke and how when she and my mother got together, you could barely understand what they were talking about because they both spoke so fast. Plus, they always felt that they knew it all and ended up getting the nickname "the professors" from my uncle Jr. Once they got going, you couldn't get a word in.

There are of course times when I think of my Aunt Diane, and how all of the kids and even my older cousins loved staying over at her place. Anytime we went to visit Diane, we felt so free. She let us jump on the beds, eat junk food, stay up late and just be free to be a kid. The older cousins got to eat junk food and stay out a bit later than their usual curfew, so they of course loved coming over to spend the weekend with Diane. It was also nice to get the experience of having pets because while Diane always had cats like Trixie and Mikey, my grandmother wouldn't allow us to have any pets at her home. So it was nice to share the experience with Diane and my cousins Toya, Sheron, also known as Punchy, and my cousin David.

Like Diane, my Uncle Dougie was also the type of relative that the kids and teens wanted to be around. Dougie wasn't only generous with giving us kids some spare change to buy snacks; he was also the kind of uncle who would pick us up with his car and take us for rides to do cool things like eat out for lunch and at times take us to see popular movies. I remember when he surprised me and some of my younger cousins and took us to see *Bebe's Kids*. Plus, when we stayed over at his place it was similar to when we stayed over at my Aunt Diane's apartment. We got to stay up late watching TV and got to eat junk food. So I of course loved going to spend time with Uncle Dougie.

Like my Uncle Dougie, there were other uncles who were loving males throughout my childhood. My Uncle Stanley, although rough around the edges and at times a bit scary to some of the younger cousins, was hilarious to me. I never feared Uncle Stanley. Even though he at times came across as stern, being with him made me feel protected. It was like no one would mess with us if he was around because all he had to do was give them a look. Uncle Stanley like my Uncle Dougie had served in the military. However, after suffering an injury on one of his legs, Uncle Stanley walked with a limp. Yet, he could still instill fear in anyone with the look in his eyes. However, regardless of how tough he appeared to the outside world, I will always remember the sweet times that he spent taking his daughter Kenterri and me to the Central Park pool at 110th Street. Or the times that he coached my brother and Sharday's little league teams.

Between those two uncles and my Uncle Jr., I had several interesting and protective uncles in my life. Uncle Jr. was the youngest of the siblings, and one might say a bit spoiled. He had also been the only son between my grandma and grandpa. So as the only son of my grandpa and the youngest child, it seemed that Uncle Jr. could do no wrong in my grandma's and grandpa's eyes. Nonetheless, Jr. often cracked me up with his sense of humor and easygoing personality. When Jr. met his wife Roberta, I loved visiting them. Later on during my teenage years, I used to babysit for them and at times would get to stay up late once the kids went to sleep. Roberta was always cool with me having my friends stay over, so I loved going over to visit them. Plus, during middle school I had two friends who lived in the same area that Jr. and Roberta lived in, so it was perfect.

Like spending time with my uncles, when my mother's friend Roosevelt came around I had an equally good time. Roosevelt was like my Aunt Pat regarding his personality, full of energy, always ready to have a good time, and loved fried chicken and cornbread. Like my Aunt Pat you could hear him from miles away. Even though Roosevelt was a family friend, he felt more like family. He came to our family functions, played Spades with the adults, danced with the kids and always bought plenty of snacks. He even treated us to arcades and to McDonalds. Things like going out to eat at McDonalds was a big deal back then. Since there was so many of us kids, my grandmother couldn't afford for us to eat out much, even to fast food restaurants.

Titania at Age 8; Winter of 1990 at Roosevelt's Apartment in Harlem

Titania at Age 9; Summer of 1991 at Arcade with Roosevelt & Other Family Members

I also think back to when I used to try to fit into Asia's and my other older cousin Washeka's clothing. I had a lot of good times with Asia, Washeka, whom we called Taneka, and my cousin Shauntea. They always seemed to wear the latest trends. However, since Asia lived in my grandmother's home with me and Taneka was often there, I mostly used to beg those two cousins to borrow their clothes or purses. Sometimes they would just let me borrow something of theirs without a second thought. However, when they realized how much I enjoyed borrowing their stuff, they figured out a way to make me earn it. So in exchange for wearing their stuff, they had me washing dishes or cleaning the bathroom on the days that they were supposed to do it. When wearing their clothes wasn't enough to get me to do their chores, they would pay me a dollar. Back then a dollar was a huge deal for me.

I had a major sweet tooth and one dollar used to go a long way for getting a bag full of candy. I used to get bags of Laughy Taffys, Now Laters, the Finger Pop rings, mini Snickers, Sour Patch gummies, Cry Babies gum balls, Lemon Heads, Boston Baked Beans, Charleston Chews, Sugar Daddys and even ten cent ices. If I wanted to splurge on something sweet and cold, I would at times get one of those Italian icy cups that came with a little wood spoon. I especially loved the cherry-flavored or lemon icy cups. I loved turning the frozen icy upside down, so I could first eat the crunchy and sweeter part of the icy. At times, I hid my candy bags and other sweets. Other times, I would bring my candy bag or my ices outside to look for a spot to devour them.

Between earning money from doing chores for my cousins and my Uncle Dougie being generous with giving us kids money when he stopped by to visit, most of the time treats weren't difficult to come by. However, most of the time I had to watch out for kids in the neighborhood that were looking to score my treats if I forgot to yell "no snatchies." Yelling "no snatchies" was a game that we played in the neighborhood in which if you didn't yell out "no snatchies," it meant that you would have to give away your snacks. It was silly, but everyone bought into it. It became just as serious as a game of skellies and just as much part of hanging out as playing with cabbage patch dolls or playing hop scotch, double dutch, and calling out the order to go in and yelling "God no higher." Likewise, snatchies was just as much part of childhood games as playing tag, seven eleven, and hot piece of butter, or braiding the multi-color strands of lanyards in box or barrel-stich designs. Having to deal with the game of snatchies was also as addictive yet annoying as those multi-color click clacks.

Like the sweet memories of those times, I also think back to summer days when the fire hydrant would be turned on, and how us kids would place a cup or other type of apparatus where the water came out of the fire hydrant to create a sort of sprinkler effect. All of the neighborhood kids and teens would run through it on hot summer days, as we ran around laughing and the adults watched from their seats. Or when Super Soakers first came out and no one could escape them. Between those and the small multi-color pack of water balloons, it was hard to stay dry too long during those hot summer days. I also think back to when my cousins Kenterri, Anthony, and I would be taken to the Central Park swimming pool at 110th Street. Or how dunking was such a big deal, especially with the guys. Being dunked in the pool was a bit of a love-hate experience. On one hand, it was exciting to have someone interested enough to sneak up and dunk you. However, on the other hand it often became annoying because a few guys would get carried away and wouldn't give you a break from dunking. When this happened, I used to find myself trying to catch my breath before the next dunk and trying to adjust my swimsuit top to avoid being exposed. Nonetheless, it was for the most part innocent childhood games and fun. Those summer days at the Central Park pool were always good times, and I will always have fond memories of those moments. It's memories like these that put a smile on my face, when I think of those days I spent living with my family and around the neighborhood that I called home.

Chapter Thirteen

A Different Kind of Struggle

Although I was grateful to have a home with my family and surroundings that I was familiar with, there was still a major part of my life that felt out of whack. On one hand, moving in with my grandparents gave me more stability, structure, and comfort. Moving in with my grandparents also gave more predictability to my chaotic life. Although there were moments of uncertainty, being with my grandparents certainly reduced the anxiety over what would happen to me, more so than the life I had been living with my mother. I no longer had to worry about having enough food, living in different shelters, missing school, or being with my mother when she went to different crack spots to get high.

However, at times living with my grandparents brought about a life full of a different set of issues. Sharing a home with my grandparents also meant not having enough personal space. Like me and my younger brother David, our cousins lived with our grandparents because their parents couldn't care for them. Within my grandparent's home there were two older cousins, James whom we all called Patrick who was seven years older than me and Alisha whom we called Asia who was five years older than me. They had practically been babies when they entered foster care and came to stay with my grandmother. In addition to those two cousins, there were two younger cousins, both siblings: Aaron who is three years younger than me, and Sharday who is six years younger than me, the same age as my brother David, just months apart.

It always seemed that my cousins had a closer bond with my grandmother. I often attributed this to my cousins having been with her longer, or perhaps because my grandmother felt that they needed her more. In addition to Patrick and Asia who had been adopted by my grandparents, and Aaron and Sharday who were still in foster care, there were always other family members at my grandparent's apartment. My grandparent's home included relatives like my cousin Sparkle or cousin Tisha who would occasionally stop by to visit, as well as cousins who would stay with us when things weren't working out with their mother or father. Living with so many relatives came with its own set of complications. I can remember feeling lost in the mix. I won't say that it was awful because being around people who knew and cared about me was and remains very important to me.

Living with my cousins definitely brought about plenty of moments in which we shared laughter along with our tears. Being part of a big family helped me feel connected to people, when I needed it the most. Likewise, it was like we shared a bond based on the mutual loss of our parents and what we perceived as a normal family life. Yet, living with so many people also made it easier for me to hide. I was able to hide from the reality of my loneliness. I could also hide from the insecurities that I had developed from living a life that seemed so different from the normal life I perceived my peers had. When I was in my grandmother's apartment, it didn't feel like I had to face up to the world outside.

Yet with so many family members to get lost in, it also meant that I didn't feel special. I never felt like I had been the apple of anyone's eye. I am not sure if not feeling like I was number one in my mother's or father's eyes caused this feeling, or if living in a sea of other people caused it. Perhaps like many complicated things, it was probably a combination of factors. Either way, this at times made me feel small and insignificant. I didn't feel worthy of exploring who I was or figuring out what my dreams were. There was very little room for my dreams to grow. It also felt like no matter how much I wanted to explore my talents, there was no one with the time to give my dreams a chance to flourish. There were perhaps too many of us for my grandmother to individually help us discover and develop our dreams. I am sure she wanted to, but in many ways it was too much. There seemed to be plenty of other things to focus on. After all my grandmother had spent her childhood looking after her own siblings, and now she was spending her elderly years caring for her grandchildren. Yet, she had to deal with the daily responsibilities of caring for us, and for her children who would enter into her life when they needed something from her. But the daily caring for us was plenty on its own. Not only did she have to make sure that we all had enough food and clean clothing, but she also had to ensure that we were taken to our many appointments. Everything from court appearances to medical and therapy appointments, she made sure that we attended them all. So I certainly don't blame her for not being able to individually see that each of us focused on our dreams and life goals.

Taking me to receive individual therapy, like the other appointments, became something else that we had to do as a result of being in foster care. The first time I received counseling services outside of school I was seven years old. I remember taking the bus along with my grandmother to Harlem Hospital. I was told that between the change of being taken away from my mother and of losing a brother, my grandmother was told that I needed to receive individual counseling. So as a child I obliged and went along with my grandmother, as I talked about my feelings. However, it was hard for me to see the benefits of any of this at the time because it felt more like a juggling act of how much of myself I could share with my therapist; a person who despite the frequency I went to meet with always felt like a stranger to me. It was nearly impossible for me to feel at ease and to be myself, when all I feared was that I would say the wrong thing and that I could ruin everything. I not only feared that I would be separated from my brother, but that it would also affect my cousins who were also in foster care living with our grandparents. So even at the age of seven, I felt like I had the world on my little shoulders. At that age, therapy didn't feel like a free time where I could explore and learn. I in fact wouldn't see the benefits of therapy until my mid-teenage years, when I felt a bit freer to express myself. However, as a child, it felt like a waste of my time and a place where I had to be on pins and needles. Yet still I played the part of playing with the dollhouse that was in my therapist's office and drew the pictures of a happy family surrounded by flowers. Yet inside, I was full of fear, anxiety, and pain.

As a kid telling my story to social workers and case workers became just as routine as it was when I went to therapy. Many times the words that I spoke to social workers and other child welfare workers in fact felt rehearsed. On one hand I remember telling them what I thought they wanted to hear, like how things were going at school and on-the-surface stuff about how it was living with my grandparents. However, during that time I never felt that I could trust social workers or other child welfare workers, especially after being taken away from my mother and having spent time away from my family. In my eyes they were all part of the same system, and none of them seemed to be on my side. I had also kept the memory of the child welfare worker who lied to me about my brother and me going to the same foster home. So while I gave them the updates they needed for their jobs, I became quite skilled at keeping the parts of the most private things that were going on in my life buried in the walls of my grandmother's home. There was a great deal of mistrust, and my family always made it clear that there were certain things that I needed to keep quiet. Things such as any spankings I received, and of course the sexual abuse I experienced at the hands of Darren. However, at the time keeping secrets confined to the walls of my grandmother's home seemed like the best solution for staying close to my family and having any chance at a somewhat normal life.

When the workers came to conduct school visits, I would meet with them in the hallways of the school or sometimes the office of one of my guidance counselors. During grade school this wasn't a big deal for me, but by the time I entered middle school I hated the idea of other students asking why I was being taken out of class. I remember seeing other students in the hallway while meeting with one of the workers and of them later asking me who I was meeting with. I often lied to them about the person and would often say that it was a relative. I was too embarrassed to tell them that I was in foster care and that workers were coming to check up on me. I desperately wanted to fit in and be like everyone else, so telling them something that would make me appear different didn't feel like an option.

Titania at Age 11-Local Shop in Neighborhood

I remember that my first year of middle school was particularly difficult because of this. A new school, new surroundings, a new set of people to meet, the pressures of wanting to be liked, all mixed with the other stressors of having to explain why social workers or case workers had to visit me at school. Those feelings made me feel insecure and of course added to my feelings of being anxious about how much I should be telling the workers. I couldn't escape my fear of saying the wrong things by revealing what was actually taking place in my life. Still, as many secrets as I had to keep during those years, it somehow didn't seem as bad as the idea of being taken away from my family again.

Like my fear of saying the wrong thing, I also feared that if my grandparents became ill to the point that they couldn't care for us, that my brother and I would be taken away again. At the time, there were no aunts or uncles who could care for my brother and me. My father had never really taken much of an interest in me. Later on in life, he told me that he and my mother had been neighborhood friends as teens and that their relationship ended up becoming sexual. However, when my mother became pregnant when they were just twenty, he told her that he wasn't ready to be a father. He had asked my mother to have an abortion, but she told him that she wasn't willing to have an abortion.

However, since I didn't fit into his plans, he therefore didn't make any effort to be a part of my life other than the times that his parents forced him to be. I actually had more of a relationship with my paternal grandmother Vordie Lopez and with my paternal grandfather Francisco Lopez than I did with my own father. On many occasions if it wasn't for them telling him to visit me or them having me over at their place, I am not sure how much I would have seen my father. My paternal grandmother even did things like prepare meals for fundraisers at school events, and even helped to pay for my school pictures one year. She and my grandfather did what they could to show me that they cared and that I was a part of their family.

Even my father's sisters and brothers did their part to show that they wanted to know me and assured me that they would be there to support me; in particular, my Uncle Zaram, Uncle Donnie and Aunts Glynnis and Catalina. They definitely did their part to make sure I knew my cousins and that I felt part of the family. Yet, my father never participated in anything during this time that didn't fit into his plans or that cramped his style. During the time that I was taken away from my family and placed in a foster home he claimed that he told my mother that I could come live with him, but that my younger brother couldn't. My mother refused to have us separated, so she instead asked my grandmother to take us in. So I knew that if I said anything that would get my brother and me removed from our grandparent's home, this meant that I was going to be placed with a father who didn't seem to care what happened to me and that I would be away from my brother. Or it meant that I would be sent to another foster home with strangers, and perhaps this time for good. So the fears that I would say or do something wrong and be taken away were always lurking around the corner. These concerns were always there and made most of my childhood a very unpredictable and an unsettling time.

Needless to say, focusing on school like many other things in my life became a juggling act. I often daydreamed about a better life and escaped into my thoughts of a better way to live. During middle school I would have teachers tell my grandmother that my daydreaming was a concern to them. However, it was my way to cope with the harsh reality that I couldn't share with anyone else. I also remember watching plenty of television shows about kids who had the type of family that I wanted. I particularly enjoyed watching shows with children that lived in two parent homes and teens that seemed to possess a sense of confidence and freedom that I longed for. Shows like, *The Cosby Show, Family Matters, The Fresh Prince of Bel-Air* and *Beverly Hills 90210* were among my favorites.

Even though I didn't live the lifestyle that was portrayed on screen, I watched the shows because most of the kids and teens seemed to have loving parents and healthy bonds with their friends. The kids were able to be free to explore their interests and figure out who they were. Their troubles seemed to be everyday childhood or teenage troubles, nothing like the life I had. Even though I used those shows to escape, I at times found myself feeling a bit jealous. I remember an episode in *The Cosby Show* when Denise got the opportunity to design a shirt, and even though the sleeves were uneven, she was still excited that she was able to create it. Mr. Huxtable complained about how she wanted to do a bit of everything and how she never stayed with one thing. I remember how envious I was of Denise for getting to live a life in which she had opportunities to explore her talents. It was things like this or even the financial freedom they seemed to have to go out with their friends that I longed for. I also wanted to have a household where I didn't have to explain to my friends why my mother and father weren't around and why I lived with so many family members. Even though in shows like *Fresh Prince of Bel-Air* when Will lived with his cousins, he still had a mother who continued to be involved in his life. Or on *Family Matters* when their grandmother lived with them, it still wasn't like she had been raising them. Laura and Eddie and their younger sister Judy still had their parents looking after and guiding them. So during this time I remember wanting to live a different life and wanting to be anyone other than who I was. I no longer wanted to exist in a life where my mother was roaming the streets using drugs or where the fear of losing my grandmother meant that I would lose ties with everyone close to me.

Like the shows that I watched, school also became a way to distract me from my home life. During grade school I was always yearning to develop friendships with people that I thought could at best temporarily take me away from the part of my life that I dreaded. I was always aware that I couldn't invite just anyone to sleep over at my grandparent's apartment, mainly because we didn't have enough space for anyone else. However, it was also because I didn't feel comfortable sharing with everyone why I lived with my grandparents. However, this didn't mean that I couldn't sleep over at a few of my friends' homes. As long as my grandparents knew the parents and felt comfortable with me sleeping over, I was on occasion allowed to escape to enjoy a sleepover.

During grade school I tried as much as possible to fit in. I even joined a leadership group during this time. Once a week during lunch we met and discussed ways to improve the school, volunteered, and fundraised. Our volunteer experiences pertained to helping the kindergarten classes during their recess. We would do things like assist the teachers in watching the younger kids, and helped to put away the toys that were brought out to the play yard. We also helped to get the younger kids back in their class once their lunch period was over. To fundraise we sold chips and pretzels during our lunch break. Participating in activities like this at school not only helped to keep my mind off of my worries, but they helped me to make friends. I tried doing as much as possible to get away. Since I had always liked to dance, I joined a dance club that allowed me to stay after school to practice. I participated in talent shows and did whatever was needed to remain outside of my home and to have some chance of feeling like a normal kid.

However, as much as I tried to escape the reality of how things were at home, my distractions only went so far. All I had to do was go home where there was always some reminder of me being a foster kid. If I wasn't reminded of some appointment that I had coming up with a case worker, I had to hear about my mother's latest attempt to sign herself into a drug treatment program. Yet those stays were always brief, and my grandmother would end up telling me that my mother didn't finish the program. My grandmother would find out from one of my aunts or uncles who had seen my mother hanging out on the streets again and heard about her getting high. So my happiness about my mother's recovery was often short lived and broke my heart every time. Even though I was aware of her many attempts, I wanted so bad to believe that each time would be the time when she would turn her life around. I couldn't give up the hope that I would one day have my mother back, and that I would have the kind of life that I saw on shows like *The Cosby Show.* Well, maybe not to that extent, but some version of that.

Yet everything at school didn't help me to forget the life I lived outside of those school walls. When I was in class without the distractions of the good times I shared with my peers, I found it very difficult to concentrate on school. I was also very ashamed that I had a difficult time reading and hated when I was called upon to read aloud. So instead of being mentally present or focused on my academics, I found myself daydreaming about the life I wanted. I needed relief from my constant worries about where my mother was, or if I would see her again, if someone would find out about the sexual abuse, or if my grandmother would die. After all it wasn't hard for me to think of unexpectedly losing people through death. At the age of seven I had already lost my brother Marquis to Sudden Infant Death Syndrome (SIDS) and when I was nine I had also lost my grandpa from what seemed to come out of nowhere. After falling during a hospital visit, grandpa suffered a concussion and internal bleeding that would later lead to his death just weeks after his fall. Just as I had been in a state of disbelief from the loss of Marquis, losing grandpa also made losing people seem like something that I wasn't ready to fully process at that time. All I could think of was how easy it all seemed that someone so close could be ripped out of my life. I tried to think of the good times that we had shared, but somehow they often only reminded me of what I was missing and had lost. It also made my fear of losing everything even more real and heightened my already intense fear of returning to foster care if something similar happened to my grandma.

So creating a fantasy world where none of this existed seemed like a better alternative than the reality of being present in class. Besides, at the time I couldn't understand how my education would help me escape my life. So despite my potential, I found a way not to focus on school while appearing to be focused. Instead of daydreaming into space I ended up sitting up straight, crossing my hands and daydreaming while I looked at the teachers. Yet this only got me so far, because while I appeared to be focused I was off in a different world. So while my behavior wasn't an issue, academically I struggled. When things were relatively stable at home I was fully present, but my concentration fluctuated like the events at home.

However, during the 7th grade my mother had signed herself into a drug treatment program. Yet, unlike the outpatient programs that she had often entered and dropped out of, this was a long-term inpatient program. I will admit that I initially didn't know how to feel about this. While I had always kept a sense of hope that she would stop using drugs, I had also experienced several times prior to this that I was disappointed. Still I kept hold of the dream that she would get herself together and that I could one day live with her again. I thought that maybe, just maybe I could have what I felt was a normal life.

During the beginning of her stay at the drug rehabilitation center it was hard on me because she wasn't allowed to have visitors. Eventually she earned family visits, and my brother and I were therefore able to visit her. It was strange to see my mother in a drug treatment facility, but it was certainly better to know that she was no longer roaming the streets using drugs. It was also nice to see her looking healthy and seeming fully present when she met with my brother and me. I remember thinking to myself that my brother and I finally had a mother who was willing to fight for us.

However, when she earned a weekend pass I was once again put in a state of uncertainty and fear. As much as I wanted to be happy that she had earned the right to be out for a weekend, I still wondered if she would find herself back with the same crowd of people that had supported her drug abuse in the past. I was tired of competing with them, the streets, and crack for my mother. I needed to have her back in my life. When my mother didn't relapse I not only started to gain a sense of trust in her, but also in the world around me. I became more open with friends at school and even confided in a friend of mine about where my mother was staying. My performance at school improved, and for the first time I was on the honor roll. Things seemed to be heading in the right direction until my grandmother passed away from a heart attack two days before my middle school graduation.

Once again, my world was up in the air and nothing seemed real. My grandmother had been so many things to me and had kept me together when no one else stepped up to do it. She had been my support system, and had given her last years to provide a home for me, my brother, and endless cousins. Despite the large number of family members that I had to share her with, I had come to see that we each had a different kind of bond with her. However, just as she had been so many wonderful things to me, I also knew that she had meant so much to my mother. So I also feared that losing my grandmother would also mean losing my mother.

While losing my grandmother took an emotional toll on everyone, my mother didn't relapse. My mother instead continued to remain clean of drugs and worked toward taking the family court mandates set to regain custody of my brother and me. Since my sister Tiffany had already been adopted, we were told that she couldn't come to live with us. I remember feeling that everything seemed to be happening so fast that I felt lost. I no longer knew where I fit in or how my new life would be. Yet I sensed that I needed to find a way to adjust to what kind of life was ahead.

Even though my brother and I had been able to remain in my grandparents' apartment, my mother moving back into the apartment took some time to adjust to. The home suddenly went from being full of family members to feeling like a home to just a few people occupying the apartment. Even though my mother was added to the lease, my cousin Patrick had remained the head of the household according to the housing subsidy that we received to pay most of the rent. So he continued to live there, along with my brother and me. By this time my older cousin Asia had moved out, and following my grandmother's passing away my younger cousins Sharday and Aaron had to live with our Aunt Diane. So even though I was regaining my mother, it felt like I had also lost so much.

Coping with the loss of my grandmother and the emptiness of a home that was once filled with so many family members was more difficult than I had imagined. The loss of my grandmother was the biggest hit that my family had experienced and definitely overshadowed a time that was supposed to be filled with happiness over being reunited with my mother. Not to mention the adjustment it was for me to live with my mother and to have her go from being more a friend to now being a parent. For many years I resented her and wanted to express my hurt, but instead I kept things inside out of fear of her relapsing. There was so much left unsaid about my feelings of being abandoned by her and not feeling protected for so many years. Forget talking about the sexual abuse. Yet we both did our best to carry on as if none of those things had happened.

It took everything I had to adjust to my new life with her. I often compared her to my grandmother, from little things like how she cooked to how emotionally distant my mother seemed. While my grandmother was always affectionate toward me, my mother barely even gave me a hug. When she hugged me, it felt artificial and rigid. It seemed like we were both uncomfortable in our new roles, and it only made me miss my grandmother even more. Looking back, I definitely wish we had received family therapy following our reunification. Being able to talk about how the transition affected us could have broken down the wall that continued to grow out of our lack of communication and avoidance of issues that we could have faced head on. Instead we existed in world where we acted out of frustration, hurt and the pain over what had taken place during the years that my mother was held by the world of drugs.

On the other hand, I had continued to find ways to escape. One way that I had learned to get attention at an early age was from males. I suppose being an attractive teenager made it all too easy to find guys that could provide a means of escape from the reality of my life. So between what I had learned from the sexual abuse and the attention I seemed to get from guys, I spent several years losing myself in the guys that I dated. I ended up spending a number of years escaping into the arms of the opposite sex. I even lost my virginity when I was just 11 years old. The first time I had sex was in a staircase of my grandmother's apartment building. I was only a child and was still wearing panties that had the days of the week written on them, yet I had sex. His name was Joey, and though he was only 13 years old, Joey was very good at persuading me that we should have sex.

There was a major part of me that knew that I was too young to share my body in that way. Yet I had been so insecure and concerned about losing Joey that I went along with what he asked of me. At the time, losing Joey felt like I would be losing a part of me. After the sexual abuse I had endured as a child, I had developed a false understanding about love, self-worth, and sexual relations with men. At that very impressionable age, I had confused my feelings and thoughts and believed that having sex with Joey would bring him closer to me. I figured that having sex with him would bring us so close that he would have no choice but to love me.

I can remember the evening that Joey and I had sex like it was just last year. Joey started by bringing up the topic and asking me how much I knew about it. I pretended to have some idea of what people did during sex and had told him that I tried it once before. However, during this time kids my age were talking about sex as if everyone had tried it. It's so hard to believe looking back, but we spoke about sex in grade school as if we had a clue of what it was about. So telling Joey that I had had sex once before felt like the cool thing to say, especially since he was a little older than me.

After our conversation about having sex, Joey finally asked if I wanted to have sex with him. I had told him that I wanted to get to know him more before I did it, but he didn't let up. It seemed like every time we hung out he brought up the topic of sex. It didn't matter what we had started the conversation about, it somehow always led to him asking about how my first time was or some aspect of sex. Even if we spoke about going to the park, he found a way to ask if I would ever try having sex in a park. I could have probably brought up any topic including going to church and he would have found a way to connect it to sex. Finally after his constant attempts to get me to talk more about sex he asked me once again if I would have sex with him. He spent a week asking and convincing me that he cared about me and that this would help our relationship. Part of me was curious, but a major part of me was terrified. Nonetheless, I agreed to have sex with him.

When the day to have sex finally came, I wasn't sure if I could actually go through with it. So I told Joey that I would meet him in the stairwell after going to wash up. Joey agreed to meet me, but was also sure to let me know that if I changed my mind he would lie and tell everyone that I had had sex with him. At the age of 11, I was deadly afraid of something like that getting back to my grandmother, so I kept my promise to him and showed up.

We met in the stairwell on the 25th floor and we walked up two flights to the 27th floor. Joey took the lead and told me to sit down, and I did as he told me to. He then asked if I wanted to take off my shorts or if I wanted him to do it. I sat there uncomfortable and uncertain, but I just let him strip away my clothes as he stripped away what I had considered to be the rest of my sexual innocence. As he proceeded to remove my shorts, my heart raced, my palms were clammy, and I became so nervous that I started to tremble. I was sure that he could see how nervous and reluctant I was, but I could also see that he could care less. All he was concerned with was having sex, and perhaps the fear of being caught in the act, especially by someone who knew us. The only moment that somewhat helped to relax me a bit was when he had discovered that I was wearing the days of the week panties. This made him laugh and helped me to let out a nervous laugh.

Right before we were about to have sex, I asked if he had any protection and he asked if I had my period yet. I told him no and he said, "so then you can't get pregnant." I was so immature that I didn't even consider the other risks I was putting my health in. So I allowed him to have sex and lay there while we engaged in intercourse. Even though the act of having sex and the physical pain only seemed to last for a few moments, the emotional stress that came after took a toll for many years following that day. After Joey and I had had sex I pulled my panties and shorts back up, and I walked down the two flights of stairs and went home. As I entered my grandmother's apartment, an incredible wave of guilt and feelings of being dirty came over me. Those feelings seemed very familiar to me, and it dawned on me that they were the feelings that I had experienced after being molested by Darren.

After that evening, Joey and I broke up because once he had gotten what he wanted, he didn't care about my feelings. It turns out that he would end up spreading what we had done around the neighborhood anyway, and it consequently got back to my older cousins. My cousin Asia ended up confronting him and helped to defend me. She told people that he had lied about us having sex, but I had already told her the truth. So she had just been covering for me in an attempt to protect me from the rumors that would spread around. I later confronted Joey about telling people what we had done, but the damage had already been done. Not only did Joey spread my personal business around the neighborhood, he also ended up dating someone that I had been friends with. In one summer I had lost my virginity, had the neighborhood find out, and had been betrayed by someone I thought was my friend. Yet this was all taking place before I hit adolescence. It turns out that between the sexual abuse and my early sexual encounter, these events would set the tone for later relationships with men and my view of self-worth.

Like when I met a guy who I will refer to as Randy, a 28 year-old guy whom I dated and became intimate with when I was just 15. We had met at a laundromat after he noticed that I couldn't find my dryer sheets. After offering to provide me with some of his dryer sheets he started flirting with me. When I look back, I think that he probably took mine just so that he could strike up a conversation. Nonetheless, before I knew it he had given me his number.

I eventually hung out with Randy at his place. He lived just around the corner from the laundromat and just across the street from where I lived. Even though Randy was aware of my age, this didn't stop him from eventually having sex with me. Randy and I carried on with this type of relationship for months until, in a jealous fit, things took on a physically abusive nature. I had been using his computer one night to chat online, and Randy misunderstood a conversation I had with another guy. We began to argue and Randy became so angry that I didn't recognize him. He was no longer the gentle and sweet guy that I had perceived him to be. His tone and facial expressions changed so drastically that I became frightened. When I told him that I was leaving, he grabbed my arm. I was so scared that I ran out of his apartment but he started to run after me. When Randy caught up to me in the hallway, he was very apologetic. He promised that he would never do anything to harm me and that he was just afraid of losing me. That night, even though Randy and I had eventually talked about what happened, I realized how possessive he was. His behavior started to worry me, especially when I started to suspect that he was following me. One day I told my concerns to a school counselor. As we spoke, I disclosed to her the nature of my relationship with Randy along with his age. In the past, I had told counselors about my relationships, so I had no idea what was to come following me sharing this with her. However, the counselor informed the authorities along with notifying my mother.

When my mother found out that I had sex with Randy, she was in a state of disbelief. Up until that point she had thought that I was a virgin. Her knowing that I had sex not only terrified me but also made me feel uncomfortable because we had never discussed sex, nor had we dealt with anything of this nature since the sexual abuse. Even after the sexual abuse had stopped, we had never discussed the issue. So when she found out about Randy, I sensed that our relationship would change.

Up until that point, even though the sexual abuse was something that I am sure came into her mind at times, it was like the memories of it suddenly all became even more present. Yet, I tried as much as I could to separate this incident from the sexual abuse. Also, unlike the sexual abuse where nothing had been done to my abuser, my mother made it clear that she wanted to have criminal charges filed against Randy. Even though the last thing I wanted was for things to unfold the way they did, I was happy to see that she was going to do something about it. There was definitely a part of me that finally felt protected by my mother. I saw a side of her that I had rarely ever seen, and it made the many sacrifices I had made sort of seem worth it. Following Randy's arrest my relationship with him ceased to exist.

While being with guys like Joey and Randy gave me a temporary escape from my life, when the reality of what I had done sunk in, the feelings of guilt and of being dirty would always come over me. Even after I spoke of the sexual abuse and my relations with men in individual and group therapy, I continued to struggle with how the abuse became so intertwined with how I saw my sexuality and my self-worth. Even though I had the opportunity to confront my abuser at a family function at the age of 17, and as powerful as I felt telling him off, I still felt that what he did would find a way to remain with me. As I suspected, the aftermath of the sexual abuse and the other relationships that followed did stay with me. The relationships that I engaged in during this time of my life led to me focus more on pleasing guys or existing in their world than developing my talents and figuring out where I fit in within this world. It was also as if following each of those relationships I regressed deeper into a world of abuse and into many situations that opened me up to new incidents of abuse. Each one made it feel more and more acceptable to be treated like less than who I actually was. So unfortunately for me, in order to cope with the memories of my past I continued to run into situations that, as bad as they were, provided a sense of escape from the memories of my childhood.

When I wasn't looking for guys to escape into, I found new ways of trying to leave behind the harsh reality of my life. A life that by high school I had to deal with without the support I had once had from my grandmother. A life with my new reality of living with a mother who found it so difficult to talk about and deal with our past that she pretended it hadn't existed. Instead, my mother escaped deeper into her own world with a guy who I will refer to as Rob whom she had met while she was in the drug treatment program. However, unlike the daydreaming I had done during middle school, I had learned during high school how easy it was to cut school. Some days I would pretend to head to school, but I would actually just ride the subway. Or I would attend some classes during the morning and cut out of my afternoon classes.

However, it was during the 10th grade that I met an English teacher who saw something in me. Mr. Berger inspired me to dig deeper into myself and to also feel comfortable to share who I was with others through my words. I felt so connected to him and actually developed a crush on him. I even wrote a letter to him explaining how I felt, but of course him being the responsible adult that he was, he instead did something that would later have such a great impact on my education and overall life. I suppose my letter showed my desperation for someone to care for and look out for me. So Mr. Berger linked me to a mentoring program within the school that was affiliated with The Financial Women's Association. The association consisted of a group of accomplished women who were volunteering their time to mentor young girls within my high school. The program helped to expose me to a world that I wouldn't have typically been exposed to, including cultural activities involving the arts. We were matched based on similar interest and based on who the school coordinator felt would be a good fit. We all met after school in the cafeteria and participated in activities that allowed us to learn more about each other. I couldn't have been more blessed than I was when I met Gail. Prior to knowing Gail, I had been struggling at school academically due to cutting classes. Additionally, I had not felt connected to my peers at school or to my purpose for pursuing an education.

Before Gail, I had also been going through an emotionally challenging time between the loss of my grandmother and the adjustments of being back with my mother. I had been experiencing such a difficult time that I had been hospitalized for several suicide attempts. On several occasions, I had my stomach pumped of sleeping pills and anti-depressants. I had been prescribed everything from Zoloft, to Paxil, to Trazodone, to Prozac. Yet, as long as my life felt out of control I felt no desire to live. I had on several occasions spent weeks at Mount Sinai Hospital. Looking back, there were times that I actually preferred those hospital stays. I suppose it was a break from the daily noise I heard from Rob's and my mother's constant arguing. Yet, I know that it was also that when I was hospitalized with other teens who had been going through similar things, I felt less alone. Outside of the hospital I had felt different from everyone else and disconnected. Yet, inside of the hospital I felt understood and had developed a bond with the other teens. We did nearly everything together from having school lessons, to group therapy, eating meals together, and participating in recreational activities in the gym. I remember enjoying playing volleyball as well as getting a chance to paint and sketch during our art therapy sessions. At times it felt more like a vacation from the stress and loneliness that I experienced when I was back home. However, I eventually had to come to terms with coping with the reality of life outside of the hospital. So finding my mentor Gail during this time definitely helped me to connect to others, particularly my community within school.

During my junior year of high school following being introduced to Gail, things started to take a more positive turn at school. I started to become more involved in school and invested in my education. For once I started to see how I could work toward a future that I wanted with education. After working with my mentor Gail I gained a more solid direction of where I wanted to be. Gail helped me plan and take the steps I needed to get my life off the path that it was heading toward.

I started to feel more present in my life and desperately wanted to take control of things that would shape me. Gail helped to ground me particularly during my junior year of high school, when things once again started to take a turn for the worse.

It had only been three years after my mother had moved in and regained custody of my brother and me that our world was once again disrupted. I won't ever forget this period because of how traumatic the events were that led to us being evicted from the apartment. It all started during one evening that started off feeling like any other night in that apartment. I was alone in my bedroom, and my younger brother was watching TV in the living room. My mother and her boyfriend Rob were arguing as usual, but this time things became more physical between them. I heard my mother scream "get off of me," so I ran into their bedroom. Between my mother screaming, the banging against the walls and me leaving my bedroom, my brother followed me into their bedroom. However, my mother had claimed that they were just play fighting and told my brother and me to return to our rooms. Even though we weren't sure if their wrestling was playful or not, we left the room as my mother had told us to do. What seemed like just a few minutes later, we heard Rob yell out that he was bleeding. He continued to yell out that his face was cut and that he was tired of her playing around.

Rob was an aspiring musician, and I knew how much he focused on his looks. However, I had no idea how something that they claimed was playful would take such a turn. Yet, after Rob left the apartment he went to call the police to make a report. Minutes later my mother was questioned by police officers and asked if there was anyone that my brother and I could stay with. Luckily a neighbor offered to watch us until either my older cousin David or Patrick stopped by. Even though we didn't see my mother get handcuffed, I knew that they were going to take her to the precinct. However, at the time I had no idea of when she would return home and if my brother and I would once again be taken away from her. So once again things were up in the air. My brother and I sat on the neighbor's couch while she asked what had happened. David and I just cried as we worried about our mother. Other than our tears I remember continually asking our neighbor if I could check to see if one of our cousins had come into the apartment. Finally after two hours our cousin David was home, and we were allowed to return to our apartment. David stayed with us that night and awaited news about my mother. The following morning we found out that my mother was going to be released. However, our joy would be short lived.

While I was exhausted from worrying about my mother and our future, when she arrived home I suddenly felt a lot more relaxed. She started to make some breakfast for David and me, but my stomach was still unsettled from the events of the previous night. Still, once I knew that she was home I could finally sleep, so I went into my bedroom. However, I awoke to my mother telling me that we had to leave the apartment. She wasn't giving me any explanation at the time other than saying that she wasn't sure when we could return. She told me to pack some clothing, but I was still in a state of shock, so I barely packed anything. I didn't take my school books or anything other than two outfits and a pair of sneakers. After leaving the apartment, we temporarily stayed at my Uncle Stanley's apartment. However, it was clear that we were evicted from the apartment that my brother and I had spent a great deal of our lives in. Even though my mother had moved into that apartment, it always felt like my grandmother's home. Being in that apartment after she had passed away gave me a connection to her, and now it felt like the last of what I had of her was being ripped away. It became clear that we weren't returning to that apartment, when my mother told us that we were going to a shelter.

Before getting a shelter we had to go to the Prevention Assistance and Temporary Housing (PATH) office. The day we waited for our shelter turned into night and reminded me of those nights as a child that my mother and I waited to be shipped off to shelter after shelter. However, as familiar as those feelings were for me, I knew that my brother hadn't shared those experiences. So I did my best to comfort him, but he was so stressed out that he vomited. When he threw up, it suddenly reminded me of when I had done the same thing as kid. At the time it had just been my mother and I, and we ended up staying overnight at the PATH office until a shelter was found for us. In the morning we were given a meal, and shortly after eating it I felt incredibly sick. I continued to vomit on and off for most of the morning. Even till this day I still don't know if it was something I ate, or if my nerves were shot from the stress of being in that place.

While my brother, mother and I waited for our names to be called for our physicals, my mind continued to shift between the present and the many times from my past that I had experienced moving from different shelters during my childhood. I also thought of the time that my mother and I waited at a different PATH office and had been so hungry but didn't have any money. We must have arrived after they provided food because I remember my mother asking me if I would give her the 20 cents that I had in my Penny Loafers. I remember giving her a hard time initially because my Aunt Pat had given me those two dimes and told me never to take them out. When Pat had given me those dimes, I had felt so special because most kids had pennies in their Loafers. So I had promised my Aunt Pat that I would never remove them. However, that's what things were like with my mother, she had a way that made everything she needed or wanted seem to be more important than anything else. Like it had been with other things in the past, I had learned how to give up things and how to conceal my true feelings when it benefited my mother. She had a way about her, and I always felt bad about not giving her what she asked for. So I let her take the money out of my shoes, so we could buy a pack of 25 cent strawberry-flavored cream cookies. She had found four pennies between the PATH office and the corner store. The guy at the store let us get the cookies a penny short.

I remember how my mother had wanted to get the cookies with the lemon-flavored cream in the middle, but how the store was out of those. She was annoyed that they didn't have the flavor she wanted, so she let me choose which flavor I wanted. It was kind of funny how even with things that I had very little choice about, she would somehow make it seem like I had some say. I also thought about how she had promised me that she would replace those dimes, but how she never got around to it. I also remembered that I had never bothered to ask her for them. I suppose at that point I no longer felt like it was worth it, or perhaps I just didn't want to think about it that night. Then suddenly my mind was jolted back to the present day as our names were called for our physicals.

After that night we were sent to a temporary shelter in Harlem on West 145th where all three of us shared a room. There were two beds, so my mother slept in one bed, and my brother and I shared the other. The room was small and was relatively clean. One of the guys that my mother used to be involved with had given my mother a small portable TV to help David and me feel a bit more comfortable. Yet, while watching TV had in the past helped me to escape, it became increasingly difficult to tune out what my life had once again become. It seemed like I had no break from the type of chaotic way my life had been growing up. That feeling of whenever something good happens there is always something devastating right around the corner. I remember telling myself that the moment my life seemed to have some sense of normalcy to it, my home and my chance of having a normal teenage life was destroyed. Instead of just being able to study for my Regents Exams and an advanced placement exam, I had to focus on where we would live. So I had to continue on and try my best to remain focused on school, while everything around me was unstable and depressing.

After a month of living in that room we were sent to a tier two shelter in Brooklyn, where my mother was told we would remain for anything between six months to a year before an apartment could be found and approved for us. However, when we arrived, we were once again placed in one room. This time the room was filthy and even more uncomfortable than the room we had just left. We tried cleaning the room, but it was no use. The furniture had been damaged, and none of us wanted to stay there. My brother and I had no appetite and cried profusely.

Adding to our feelings of despair, some of the other residents decided to scare us and discuss how the place was filled with rodents including rats. We were so frightened and disgusted with the place that I remember breaking down in the hallway and screaming that I wanted to die. I felt as if I could no longer take what life had dealt me. After several complaints to the social workers at the shelter, we were able to find a different room with two bedrooms and a small kitchen. Even though it wasn't the home we had been evicted from, we had no choice but to make it our home. So we all did our best to clean the place and make the necessary adjustments to feel somewhat secure.

However, my sense of security wouldn't last when I later found out that my mother would be marrying Rob, so that he could come to live with us. Even though he wasn't the reason that we had been evicted from the apartment, between their constant arguing and her arrest I didn't want to see him. Plus, my mother later told me that they moved us to a Brooklyn shelter after hearing about the domestic violence incident that took place between her and Rob. So adding to the misery of the already frustrating living conditions Rob was once again back.

I tried as much as I could to just ignore him, but it was incredibly difficult in such a small place. Plus I had grown up in Manhattan, and none of my friends from school lived anywhere close to where we were in Brooklyn. Also, it wasn't like I had money to go anywhere. I wanted to spend some time staying with friends or relatives who lived in Manhattan, but when we first arrived we were told the rules of the shelter required that everyone who was living there needed to sign in at night. So I was stuck in that area with someone who had been verbally abusive to my mother and nearly caused my brother and me to be sent back into the foster care system. Although I despised Rob and detested the living conditions of the shelter, I came to accept that this was something I would have to endure for that time.

Just as I started to feel somewhat stable, there would be something else that would throw things off once again. It was an afternoon that my mother, David and I had returned to our old neighborhood to visit her brother. What started off as a friendly visit turned into yet another blow, when my mother revealed to me that we were losing our belongings that had been put in storage. She had told me that the place where our things were taken following our eviction was just a temporary storage facility. My mother explained that the place our belongings were sent to was just meant to be for 30 days, and that we needed to find another storage facility to move our stuff to. However, they were looking for us to pay to have our things removed in addition to paying for a truck for the removal. Unfortunately, my mother didn't have any money, and no one could lend her the money during the time. So she told me that everything would be auctioned off.

I hated the idea that all of our personal possessions would be sold to strangers and that our sentimental items like family photos would be discarded. Yet my mother expressed that she felt hopeless to do anything and seemed to accept that this was the way that things would be. I remember being so angry with her because it reminded me of the many times as a child that she accepted defeat, and how much we had lost along the way. To her our things had just become items that could be easily replaced, but to me those objects were a connection to my past. Some of my belongings helped to remind me of the good times that I had experienced growing up at my grandmother's place. I finally became so annoyed that I asked her if I could call the storage facility and speak with someone. She told me that she didn't think it would help because she had tried. Yet, I couldn't let our belongings go without a fight.

So I went to a pay phone nearby and pleaded with them to let us have our belongings back. At first I was told that they couldn't help us without us paying nearly a $1000. I told the woman on the line that we had no money. She said that there was nothing that she could do, but that she would check with her supervisor. I waited and finally she returned to say that we would need to pay. So I cried and asked what they would do with our pictures. I suppose hearing a child cry in such desperation hit a soft spot because she asked me to call back in an hour. When I called back, she told me that they would give us items like family photos at no charge and that they would even reduce the entire payment to $200 if we could get access to a truck and have all of our items moved by the following week. A sense of relief and excitement came over me, and I ran back to my mother to tell her about the news.

My mother called everyone she could, yet everyone continued to say that they couldn't lend her the money. Finally, the executive director of the drug rehabilitation center that she and Rob graduated from was able to get the money and get us access to a truck. I will always be grateful to Mr. James Allen for helping us during our time of need. So with his generosity, our belongings were finally going to be back where they belonged. Even though there was still a sense of uncertainty living in that shelter, it felt good to have things that reminded me of home.

Yet, life at that Brooklyn shelter seemed to last a lot longer than my mother had initially led us to believe. It wasn't long that my feelings of uneasiness and annoyance crept back up, especially with Rob and my mother constantly arguing. They were either laughing or clawing at each other's faces. It was so rare when things were in between with them that I don't recall those occasions. What I do recall are the heated arguments that exploded about why Rob would disappear from the shelter for days at a time, and where and whom he might be with during those stays. Other times, they argued over Rob relapsing on heroin and shooting up again as my mother would say. I remembered that he had done this from time to time while we were living at my grandparent's old apartment. He would check himself into the rehabilitation center that he and my mother met at and just return to her place when he felt he was better. Years later my mother admitted that she too had relapsed during this period, but that she was able to discontinue her drug use. So as if living in the desolated area in Brooklyn where the shelter was located wasn't enough, I had to witness the verbally abusive insults that Rob and my mother casually threw around while David and I sat in the room next to theirs. Yet regardless if he called her a whore or bitch, she would end up turning around an hour later and cooking dinner for him. Or they would be laughing about something.

I hated Rob mainly because of how he treated my mother, but also because he demanded so much of my mother's attention. My mother had explained to me that his mother was never involved in his life and that he spent years looking for her love and approval. So when he found my mother, a person who despite his horrible treatment toward her had stayed around, he wasn't willing to let her go. Yet, this was all taking place during a pivotal time in my brother's and my relationship with our mother. We had spent several years waiting for her to return to us from the drugs, and now we had to compete once again for what she considered to be the love of her life. The only times my brother and I had my mother's undivided attention seemed to be during the times when she received visitation with us while she was at the drug rehabilitation center. During this period my mother tried so hard to win us over and prove how much she loved us. However, once Rob came into the picture her priorities seemed to change. David and I saw less and less of our mother, and we did less together as the Three Musketeers. The Three Musketeers is what she used to refer to us as after she regained custody of us. So I both despised Rob and envied that he could have her love and affection, while my brother and I stood in the next room still waiting.

However, Rob struggled with seeing how our emotional needs from our mother needed to be met. He continued to take more and more from her, and when he learned that we had to remain in the shelter longer, he ended up bailing out on her. My mother claimed that we had to stay longer due to our housing application not being accepted. She told me that it was probably due to her getting arrested after the domestic violence report Rob had made. So now I had to live in a dirty shelter that was in the middle of nowhere on the last stop of the L train in Brooklyn. This made my hatred for Rob grow more and more by the minute; especially because Rob bailed on my mother while she was working at a fast food restaurant quite a distance from the shelter. The path that she had to walk consisted mainly of warehouses and was very deserted at night.

During the time that she worked for the restaurant she told us that a woman had been raped and shot in the area. So during the nights that she returned late from closing, Rob used to pick her up from work. However, when Rob wasn't around, my younger brother and I would go to pick our mom up from work. My mother hated the idea that my brother David and I were coming late at night and walking without any protection, but she knew that we were too worried to have her walk alone. I was always aware that anything could have happened to us during those walks, but like it had been in the past the threat of losing her always seemed to be more terrifying. I had always loved my mother and growing up felt like I had to stand up for and protect her. So in many ways I continued to feel like I was *her* mother. Of course my anxiety over being just 17 years old and not yet having finished high school, plus living within a shelter, all served as constant reminders of my earlier fears. The nagging underlying thoughts of the floor being pulled from beneath our feet pressed on my mind every night she left for work. I had no idea how my brother and I would survive or where we would live if something happened to my mother during this time.

While these years certainly helped to bring David and me closer together, they still remained some of the most emotionally exhausting and unpredictable times of my life. Yet, they will always hold a special place when I think of the times David and I stayed up talking or making up ghost stories. We often ended up being so scared that we needed to sleep in the same bed. While I loved and still enjoy a good horror story, David was always the one telling me that he didn't want to hear it, especially at night. Yet, I would somehow convince him to listen until we both became scared. I started to hear weird sounds, and then he would say that he saw something. Then we would hear a thump or some ordinary sound I am sure, but we would both jump and let out a scream. On school nights my mother used to yell out "what are you doing, go to bed." This of course made us laugh even louder, but we would still look at each other in a certain way that let the other know that we were afraid of sleeping in the dark. At first we would pull the covers over our heads, but when it became too hot, we would have to come out for air. Sometimes we would just leave a little opening for the covers so we could breathe properly. However, other times when we couldn't bear it, David would come sleep in my bed. We were so close, even though we are six years apart. Being away from everyone else definitely made us live in our own world and really pushed us to learn more about each other. Having a close relationship with David had always been important to me. Yet, in the past I had felt more like I had to protect him like a mother would do, than to just enjoy being siblings. Growing up with so many other cousins, especially in such tight living quarters meant that we at times fought each other. So if anyone ever did anything to David, I was always around to step in. I even hated seeing him get disciplined by our grandmother. I suppose most of my need to protect him was based on him being my younger brother, but a great deal also came from my fear of losing another brother.

Marquis had been just six months when he passed away from Sudden Infant Death Syndrome (SIDS). David was just a year old when Marquis passed away and was therefore too young to have any memories of him. However, I was seven years old and fully aware of his loss. Marquis was always smiling and just seemed to have a peaceful demeanor about him. When he sat in his chair that was often placed on the living room table in my grandmother's home, he would usually look around with his big dark eyes and smile at everyone. If he wasn't smiling at us, he was looking up at the chandelier and smiling. I rarely ever heard Marquis cry, but I remember that he used to vomit quite a bit. His vomiting used to infuriate my mother, partially because she had little patience, but mainly because she hadn't been in a healthy state of mind due her continued use of drugs during this time. However, even as a kid I always knew that it was the drugs that dictated her behavior. I knew how sweet my mother could be when she was clean of drugs. Besides even with the drugs, I could see how much losing Marquis affected her. After he passed away she kept his bibs, even the ones with his vomit on them. She even refused to wash them.

The day I found out that Marquis had passed away I had just returned from school, but when I rang the doorbell no one was home. I remember ringing the doorbell so many times because I couldn't believe that no one was home. This was unusual because with the number of people who lived with my grandmother or visited her on a regular basis, I couldn't believe that no one would be home. This was of course before the age of kids having cell phones, or even most adults. Plus, my grandmother was so old-fashioned that she didn't even carry a beeper.

So I had no choice but to go downstairs in front of the building and wait until I saw a family member with a key to the apartment. As I waited, my stomach grew more and more uneasy. When I saw my grandmother's oldest sister whom everyone referred to as Aunt Sister, I knew that something was wrong. Aunt Sister was in her early 80s and she rarely ever came over. Instead we would go uptown to her home to visit her. Sometimes we even stayed during weekends. So when she came over to me, I knew that something awful had happened. I asked her where grandma and grandpa were, and she said that they were at the hospital. I instantly thought that something must have happened to one of them, but my thoughts were interrupted by Aunt Sister telling me that it was about Marquis. She said that he had passed away in the apartment and that he had been taken to the hospital.

I was so confused about Marquis' death and was in a state of shock. Marquis had seemed so healthy and was so young. I couldn't understand how a baby just six months old who hadn't shown any signs of being sick could just die. It felt like it came out of nowhere and from nothing. Marquis was the youngest person I knew who had passed away and by far the closest person I had lost at the time. Hearing that Marquis had died made it clearer to me that anyone could go at any moment. His loss only heightened my already present worries that I could lose my loved ones and from things that I couldn't understand.

No one seemed to understand what SIDS was, so instead the focus went to where Marquis would go now that he had passed on. Aunt Sister had said that Marquis was going to be an angel and that he would always look over me. Thinking of his angelic face and personality made it easy for me to envision him in that way. However, it didn't stop me from missing him. I missed his big smile, even though he appeared to have such a small mouth. I missed his curly hair and big dark brown eyes and how he smelled. I thought of how he would stay up with me and my grandmother watching *The Honey Mooners*.

During his funeral he wore a white suit that my Aunt Diane had picked out. His coffin was the smallest I had seen up until that point. As he lay there, he just looked as though he was asleep. That period felt surreal and I found myself escaping into a world where he was still alive. I tried to hold on to the moments we had shared, but it became difficult between the reality of him no longer being around and my constant fear of how my mother would react to this loss.

My mother seemed to mourn the loss of Marquis by escaping deeper into her world of drugs and by avoiding the apartment. There was a significant time during which my brother and I didn't even see her. The only way we knew she was still alive was from aunts and uncles who had seen her on the streets. When she eventually came around, she at first wouldn't even come up to the apartment. We had to see her downstairs. As time went by my mother made her way upstairs, but at first could only make it to the door before running into the stairwell. I remember sitting with her while she sat there looking into space but not uttering a word. I would just sit with her and put my hand in hers. I later started to comfort her with words and would let her know that he was in a better place. As time went on my mother was able to return to the apartment, but she never spoke of Marquis. It wasn't long after Marquis had passed that she found out that she was pregnant with my sister Tiffany. Yet, with David being the only sibling who was alive and physically living with me, I became overly protective of him.

However, after my mother had regained custody of us, I no longer had to take on that role. From that point on we were able to be typical siblings who loved each other and yet annoyed each other to no end. We fought over things like why I had to clean up more or why he needed so much more attention. He complained about my mother often being able to laugh at the mischievous things I did, while he felt that he always got in trouble if he said or did similar things. He would get so upset when my mother would say that it was how I said it. I would get jealous about their bond and say that he was a momma's boy; we would end up going back and forth like siblings do, but it felt good to have those moments of normalcy.

However, when Rob returned to the Brooklyn shelter we had been staying at during my last year of high school, things took a turn for the absolute worse. I had become fed up with how Rob was treating my mother with his disappearances. He walked around like he was some type of king and like he didn't have to do anything. Yet, I had to clean up, help cook dinner, and be a full time student in my senior year. I had also been applying to colleges and trying my best to prepare for college. Yet, he was walking around cursing at my mother when she didn't give him money, or when she questioned where he was when he left her. I often thought how dare he leave and have my brother and me make those dangerous walks to pick my mother up from the fast food restaurant where she worked, sometimes until midnight. So one evening after Rob and my mother started arguing, I let him know how I felt. We got into a heated argument and he called me a bitch. I was so pissed off that my mother had allowed him to speak to me that way and didn't defend me. So that night I was told by my mother to prepare dinner, but I only cooked enough food for myself, David, and my mother. When she realized what I had done, she was so pissed off and ended up giving Rob her food. This only led to things becoming even more heated and me letting him know how immature and worthless I felt he was.

That night was a turning point and would result in me going to live with my mentor Gail during the remainder of the school year. Leaving my brother behind was the most difficult part, but I could no longer exist in the same household as Rob. I also found it difficult to look at my mother the same. I had spent so much time waiting for her to be clean from drugs, worrying about her safety, sticking up for her, and now it felt like she had betrayed me for a man. I was beyond hurt and felt like I needed to leave. Even though I at times regret that she didn't get a chance to see me off to my prom, I still struggle more with her decision not to protect me or stand up for herself.

Years later my mother explained to me that being in a relationship with Rob was so different for her because this had been the first time in her adult life that she felt that a man had loved her. Prior to Rob, she had only been with guys in order to pay for her drug addiction. So I later developed a different understanding of those events and why she endured the abuse she did from Rob. As I grew up, I realized that while there were personal struggles that Rob dealt with which caused him to behave the way he did, there were other positive qualities in him that I could see. Rob was musically talented and had an amazing voice. He sang in a choir and even got to travel throughout Europe. He was great at sketching and painting. I remember how he painted a picture on the door of my bedroom to help make the space more beautiful. I firmly believe that if we had all received family therapy during this time, all of us could have had healthier relationships with each other. Instead, we all lacked an understanding of each other's perspective and weren't equipped with the communication skills we needed to openly express ourselves in healthy ways. So, there was constant fighting for the attention of my mother to feed what we had both felt we had missed out on during our childhoods.

Chapter Fourteen

Reflection on How Much of My Childhood Factored into This

Being a social worker in child welfare has been emotionally draining. I have wondered if my personal experience of being in foster care makes it harder for me to work within this area of social work. Perhaps my past puts me at a disadvantage. I mean, I see and hear things that definitely remind me of my childhood each day, and it takes a toll on me. I will admit that at times my childhood memories make me more sensitive to the traumatic experiences I often witness of the children I have worked with. I find this interesting because when I initially thought of being a social worker, having grown up in foster care was something that I thought would give me an edge over other social workers. I thought to myself that I would understand the children more because of what I had gone through within the foster care system. I used to feel that my personal experiences of growing up in foster care would allow me to be an insider and that being an insider would give me a perspective that would help them. I figured that my personal experiences would remind me of what I needed, and that the children I worked with would have similar needs. I thought I could fill their needs because of our shared experiences. However, my thoughts of this not only came from my personal experiences of having been in foster care, but were also based on my experiences from years of receiving individual and group therapy. I had spent years analyzing my childhood and understanding how it all affected me. I was always trying to understand who I had become as a result of my struggles. I had in fact spent most of my adolescence and early adult life in therapy. So between my childhood and the insight I had gained from years of trying to understand myself through therapy, I just knew that this would do more to help than harm. I figured that between that and the tools I would get from my education it would all benefit my work with children within the child welfare system.

Instead, what I had once perceived to be my advantage started to feel like it was putting me at more of a disadvantage. Hearing about children's experiences of trauma from charts that I read, from co-workers, from discussions with supervisors, from trainings, and of course from first-hand accounts with the children all became too much. The charts for example told stories of children faced with nearly every tragedy imagined. The stories of their lives were of so many losses and traumas, that at times it felt more like I was reading fictional stories. There were progress notes, and psycho-socials filled with life stories of children left alone without food, of children being abandoned by parents who were addicted to drugs, or that had parents who were severely mentally ill. There was information that told of children who were emotionally, sexually, and physically abused.

There were reports of children who remembered the day that they had been removed from their parents and, many times, separated from their siblings. It was heartbreaking to read about kids that had their worlds ripped apart in one day. Story upon story of children having to leave everything behind and expected to start over within their foster homes. They were expected to just adapt to their new home and deal with the reality that their brothers and/or sisters were away in some other home. Sometimes their siblings were not even in foster homes, but had been placed in residential treatment centers. But it didn't stop there because there were children that didn't even know who their parents were. Some that had no idea about their biological families. Stories of children that had siblings that were separated so early that some could barely remember they had siblings. There were even children that had no knowledge that their other sibling(s) existed.

While reading about and discussing the traumas of these children is difficult enough, hearing first-hand accounts from the children takes a completely different emotional toll. There were plenty of times when I wanted to cry while they shared their life story. Yet I had to try my best to emotionally pull back enough to have some distance, while at the same time showing compassion for the many battles that they had fought. At times it felt like these children had been telling what felt like war stories. When I thought of them just being kids, I often wondered how could this be? Yet, they had been fighting battles from an early age and many of them continue to fight these battles and live with the scars. They continue to have to relive many of their experiences when new workers want to hear their story as opposed to just reading notes from their charts. Thus, their past becomes like open wounds that continue to be reopened, and for some may take nearly a lifetime to heal.

Chapter Fifteen

The Impact on the Workers

I wonder if being a social worker within the child welfare system has changed other social workers the way it has changed me. I often wonder how many of us have gone through transformations that break the ideals that we once had about changing this system. After working for two different agencies within child welfare, I have begun to see common threads that seem to take once optimistic and strong workers and turn them into tired, hopeless and seemingly weak advocates.

Month after month I have seen workers leave. For a few it's for better opportunities, but most end up leaving because they feel burnt out. They feel so exhausted from the daily grind of the child welfare system that they become depleted. I have heard quite a few of my co-workers say that they no longer feel that what they do will change anything. Some are so exhausted from the busy work of documentation and running from meeting to meeting, trainings and home visits that they have little energy for the children and families once they make it to the visits. So these visits just become another thing to do, instead of opportunities to truly serve the people we work with. Day in and day out, I've heard co-workers say that we are fighting a battle that can't be won.

Others talk about how we find ourselves living from paycheck to paycheck, and how we can barely financially support ourselves living in New York City. How can this be? I also had to ask myself, why is it that we are so busy advocating for others when we feel so hopeless about advocating for ourselves. Did we always feel this way? I know that I didn't always feel this way. Despite the difficult journey that it took for me to get here, before working in child welfare I was more hopeful. Even with my understanding that there was plenty to change within the child welfare system, I couldn't imagine how being a social worker within the system would change me. I went from seeing myself as a smart, confident, capable, and passionate woman to being a person in doubt and anxious about every move I made. I once felt good about being a social worker, I once felt good about being myself. Now, when I looked at myself, I saw an insecure, apologetic, and empty person. So empty that I had little drive to change things within my own life, let alone work toward motivating others towards positive changes in their life. What could it be that changes us into people that we no longer recognize and that pulls us so far from our original purpose? I have come to see that it isn't just the despair from the emotional, physical and sexual crimes we hear and see against the children we work with, but it is also the hopelessness that we feel from the endless and petty obstacles of a system that blocks the changes needed for these children to thrive.

Busywork

Even though documentation serves a purpose with regard to reporting the children's lives and the services they receive, there comes a point when the amount of documentation feels more like busywork. It becomes mindless and exaggerated, until the focus becomes more about the quantity of paperwork than on the quality of the work being done with the clients.

While we want to spend time preparing for our meetings including researching and brainstorming the best ways to meet client needs, we would be amazed at how little time is actually available to do this. Instead, for each client we have a laundry list of written reports that must be typed up, edited, and re-written. At times it seems like the main focus is on how well-written a progress note is rather than what the actual note is saying about the client. It slightly amused me when my supervisor commented on how well written my notes were. However, there were times when she would return progress notes for silly corrections as if I were in an English class. I mean I could be writing about a child that had gotten beaten up at school, but I would get a progress note returned to me because I put A.M. instead of P.M., or because an extra letter was accidentally typed at the end of a word. I would even get progress notes placed in my mailbox because I didn't write my initials on the progress note. Even more annoying was that instead of simply being able to correct the error on the hard copy, I had to spend time editing the progress notes in the computer program that we used for entering our notes.

We used a program called Connections that allowed our progress notes and reports about clients to be viewed internally by other workers. However, this program was a chore to get into. You had to double click the icon, enter your password, double click to log in, click on the client's name, then go to the progress notes tab. Once you got to the progress notes tab you had to enter the date, time, type of contact, who was involved, method of contact, for example, whether it was via phone or in person. If the contact was in person, the specific location had to be stated, and then you could finally type the actual note. Perhaps if there were one or two notes per client a week this would be fine. However, for every interaction we had with clients and about clients, we had to write a progress note with the date and time of the contact and what type of contact it was for; for example, whether it was a client contact or a collateral contact with school staff, a case worker, supervisor, service provider, medical staff member, or other. This was followed by what was discussed, what resulted, including what our follow up would be.

There were times when it felt like all I was doing was typing up progress notes. Each week, I had a stack of progress notes to submit to my supervisor. As I dropped off progress notes in her mailbox, there was a new stack waiting for me in my mailbox. I would have progress notes with ridiculous corrections that she often expected me to edit, reprint, and re-submit with my initials. If it was not progress notes it was Service Summary Forms (SSFs). SSFs were to be completed within five business days of a visit with a client and included a description of what took place during the visit. However, from the time I started, I witnessed a number of discussions regarding the completion of this form. It went from a simple document with around two paragraphs discussing the client visit, including any progress or obstacles the child/youth had in reaching his/her goals, to a document that required endless discussions about how it needed to be completed. There were even samples of well-written SSFs distributed during team meetings and discussions about every detail of completing the SSF. When they were submitted if the client goal wasn't written on the SSF, the form would be returned.

Having an SSF returned meant correcting it in the Office of Children and Family Services (OCFS) template as well as making the change to the progress note in Connections. Of course, both documents had to be reprinted and submitted along with the signed cover sheet we had the caregivers of the children sign for billing purposes. It was a vicious cycle of busywork that took time away from preparing for my visits with clients. Among our responsibilities associated with progress notes we also had to file these documents in our client's chart once they got returned. Due to the amount of paperwork we had to file, there was a table of contents included in each chart. However, most workers often became so inundated with paperwork that our supervisors had to schedule filing days. So we brought our client charts into a room where we sat and punched holes in the progress notes, stapled these notes, checked the sections where the progress notes belonged, and then checked to make sure the progress notes were in the correct order by month, day and time of the event. Perhaps if progress notes and Service Summary Forms were the only type of paperwork we needed to write, re-write, re-print and re-submit, this would not be so bad.

However, there were numerous forms that we had to type up including a ten-page document that was referred to as the Individualized Health Plan (IHP). Like the progress notes, the ten-page IHP had several parts that needed to be well-written and often revised. The IHP was a document that consisted of 14 written sections that included information on: Family/Caregiver, Permanency Goal, Living Situation, Physical Health, Mental Health, Alcohol/Substance Abuse, Community Service, Recreation or Leisure Time, Spirituality, Criminal Background, Education/School, Vocation or Job, and Budgeting/Money Management. Included in each of those sections were the History/ Risk Factors, Needs, Strengths and Preferences of the child/youth and medical consenter/biological parent, along with the preferences of the foster parent(s). Each of the 14 sections ranged from four to six sentences long to ten or twelve sentences for sections like the Family/Caregiver, Living Situation, and Physical and Mental Health sections of the report.

The next area of the IHP included the results from the Child and Adolescent Needs and Strengths (CANS) assessment. The CANS assessment was another step in this process that added time. Using a six-page document as a guide, we had to determine and rate the child/youth's and their caregiver's needs and strengths in several areas including Life Domain Function, Child Strengths, Acculturation, Caregiver Strengths, and Caregiver Needs. Depending on their needs, additional modules needed to be completed including the Developmental Module, Behavioral Module, Child Risk Behaviors, and Medical Modules. The scores were calculated and written on the IHP and entered into Connections. If previous CANS scores showed an increase or decrease, there had to be a description for each area in which the change took place.

The next part of the IHP consisted of 14 services of which we had to specify which ones the child/youth would use from a list consisting of: Health Care Integration, Family/Caregiver Supports and Services, Skill Building, Day Habilitation, Special Needs, Community Advocacy and Support, Prevocational Services, Supported Employment Services, Planned Respite, Crisis Avoidance, Management and Training, Intensive In-home Supports and Services, Crisis Respite, Adaptive and Assistive Equipment, and Accessibility Modifications. Additionally, we had to write why each service was selected and how the child/youth would benefit from the service. Finally the paragraph would end with the frequency of the service. If the child wasn't going to use a certain service, a description would still have to be included stating that the child/youth wouldn't be using the service at this time, along with why. A statement that specified that the service would be re-visited at a later time should it become relevant also had to be included.

In addition to the document outlining the services that the child/youth were scheduled to receive, the document also included a two-page budget for the services which often ranged from $30K to $50K per child. When the budget exceeded $51K, it had to be submitted with a note explaining why it went over the allotted budget. At times it would be approved, and other times the entire packet would be sent back. If this happened, the health care integrator would have to discuss with the family which services they were willing to reduce.

The last page of the IHP was the signature page, which needed to be signed by the case planner or case worker from the foster care agency, the youth, the health care integrator, and the medical consenter. If the biological parent was still the legal guardian they would be the medical consenter, but if not, the director at the foster care agency signed as the medical consenter on behalf of the child/youth.

Having these signatures may seem like a simple task, but it often depends on who is present for the meetings. If someone is missing, the submission of the IHP could be held up until the original copy gets signed. On several occasions where the medical consenter was the director of a foster care agency, the IHP signature page got misplaced and had to be re-sent. However, instead of just one signature I had to worry about getting three other people to sign the form all over again, just so I could send it back to the director of the foster care agency. On another occasion one of my clients had a parent who was incarcerated, but she was still the legal guardian. For each document that had to be signed, I needed to call her to describe the document, write a cover letter for the packet of forms I sent, and call to confirm that she had received the documents. Then I had to wait for this parent to sign the documents, and wait for them to be mailed back to me. Meanwhile, I had to hope that nothing got lost or misplaced in the sea of paperwork that floated around the office. As if this isn't exhausting enough, before the actual IHP is submitted to ACS it has to be reviewed by a supervisor, edited, re-written, emailed, plus at the request of certain supervisors, reprinted to of course make their lives easier. The dance of the IHP completion is a long and tedious process.

Again, perhaps if it stopped there that would be fine, but it doesn't. After the clients are referred to the program, the health care integrator (HCI) gets 14 days to coordinate the Preliminary Meeting. Participants of this meeting include the HCI, the HCI supervisor, the case planner (CP) or case worker (CW) from the foster care agency, the child/youth if they are ten years of age or older, the biological parents if they are still the legal guardian(s), along with the foster parent(s). However, with so many people to get together and everyone's schedule being so jam packed with meetings, trainings, client visits, the child/youth being in school, and/or the work schedule of the parents, finding a time that works for everyone can be time-consuming. There are times when several emails go back and forth for a week or more just so that everyone can agree on a good time and place to meet. Then there are times when a day before the meeting, or sometimes even the day of the meeting, you find out that the case planner or case worker can't participate. Sometimes if the parent(s) can't make it, the meeting has to be rescheduled or held in two parts. This is certainly the case when foster parents and biological parents don't get along with each other. However, when things finally come together, the Preliminary Meeting is finally held.

During this meeting the program is described by the HCI, including the services that are available. The HCI gathers additional background information about the child/youth while the HCI supervisor writes the information on the Meeting Participation Form (Blue Form). The Blue Form is a form with the names and signatures of the attendees of the meeting and the background information of the child/youth. The form is broken down into the same sections as the IHP and serves as the framework for the information that will later be typed up on the IHP. In addition to collecting the information, the HCI and HCI supervisor work with the child/youth, legal guardian(s), foster parent(s) and the foster care agency's case planner or case worker to discuss which services would benefit the child/youth. The amount of time for each service is allotted, and a tentative schedule is created. If all parties needed are present, the large list of consent forms can be signed during the meeting. Following this meeting the HCI needs to complete the Preliminary IHP packet. The packet consists of the Preliminary Check List, a progress note describing the Blue Form, the IHP, signed consent forms, scores from the CANS evaluation and a Contact Sheet with the providers from the program chosen and assigned to work with the family.

Included in the Preliminary IHP packet are Detailed Service Plans (DSPs) that need to be written for each of the services that the family and the case planning team from the foster care agency select. DSPs consist of a three-page document that at times ends up being four pages outlining the goals for each service. There is enough space for four goals, and most of the time my supervisors encouraged me to have between three and four goals. However, it typically ranged between two and four goals per service. The first page includes the client's basic identifying information, such as name, date of birth, gender, Medicaid identification number, and date of enrollment into the program.

For each DSP we had to specify which service it was for along with writing out the two to four goals for the service. The second page of the DSP included sections A and B. For section A we had to write the intervention strategy or strategies we would use or recommend to the waiver service provider to use for each goal. For section B we had to describe what the service provider staff would do to plan for the accomplishment of the goal. The third page consisted of Part 2 in which for each of the goals established, an explanation of why the goal was established or attained, or why it should be revised or discontinued had to be written. In addition to the goals, we had to specify whether the goal was new, attained, continued, revised or would be discontinued. Along with that, the status of the goal and the date each goal was established had to be included.

During the preliminary phase writing DSPs is annoying because, since the waiver service provider isn't assigned at this point, the health care integrator is responsible for writing all of the DSPs. So if the client's family and case planning team chose six to eight services, the HCI would have to write a DSP for each of those services.

If the clients get enrolled in the program, a new meeting has to be scheduled. When the initial meeting is scheduled, an additional person is required to attend. The other person who is expected to attend this meeting is the waiver service provider manager. Additionally, a new CANS evaluation needs to be conducted along with the submission of a new IHP packet following the meeting. The benefit is that the bulk of the IHP is written and only has to include the updated information. The downside is that once again everyone needs to coordinate busy schedules in order for this meeting to take place. Additionally, the legal guardian once again has to sign a new set of consent forms like the forms just signed a month ago during the Preliminary Meeting.

Once again the HCI, HCI supervisor, WSP manager child/youth, case planner/case worker, legal guardian, and foster parent(s) discuss the program and services. A new Blue Form is completed by the HCI supervisor which details Family History, Current Living Situation, School, Mental Health, Physical Health and the other areas included in the IHP. A schedule is created for the services, and the child/youth, legal guardian(s), and caregiver(s) are invited to a Meet and Greet. A Meet and Greet is an event where the new waiver service providers (WSPs), the people who will be providing the services such as Skill Building, Family Caregiver Supports and Services, Planned Respite, or any of the other available services to the child/youth are present. It's sort of a like speed dating, where the WSPs are at tables and the families are given a specified amount of time to interview the prospective WSPs and decide on which WSPs they want to work with. The health care integrators are mandated to attend this event. If the families don't attend the Meet and Greet, the HCI is expected to attend on their behalf and interview the prospective WSPs. Most of the time that is what ends up happening, so we are expected to put in overtime in order to attend the event and interview the WSPs.

However, since families who attend get first pick, when the families don't attend the event, the HCI has to plead with the WSP manager to advocate for the WSP that we want to work with our family. When we are lucky, we get a qualified WSP who works well with the family. When we are less fortunate, we get WSPs that drain us and annoy the foster parents or legal guardians. While I had some WSPs who were knowledgeable and put in a great deal of work, there were others who needed to be spoon-fed regarding the intervention strategies to use with clients. Besides that, there were others who were incredibly difficult to reach for client updates.

Chapter Sixteen

Issues with Waiver Service Providers

Having issues with WSPs wasn't only annoying, but it also added to the already demanding requirements of this line of work. There was one WSP who worked with Cari and during a visit with Cari, the WSP received a notebook from Cari's mother in which Cari expressed that she no longer wanted to live. Instead of calling me, her supervisor, or anyone from the program that we worked for, the WSP decided to write this information in a progress note, a progress note that she took a week to submit. How alarming it is to have a teen say that she doesn't want to live, yet have it be taken so lightly. According to the WSP, Cari said that she wasn't feeling that way during the time of her visit, and therefore the WSP felt that there wasn't a need to notify anyone of this information following her visit. Yet, the WSP wasn't a social worker, a psychologist, a psychiatrist or any other type of mental health provider. However, this didn't stop her from thinking that her one question about Cari's safety and her intentions to harm herself was enough for an assessment. Nor did the WSP think that this was something that warranted a phone call to me, or even to her own supervisor. She instead took an entire week to let us know about this via a progress note.

There were others who were a bit more logical but still not as efficient as was needed for this type of work. There were a few who didn't follow the goals set on the Individualized Health Plans, but instead decided to work on what they felt needed to be done during the visits. Needless to say the children weren't progressing on the goals being set, yet I would have to hear the complaints from their foster parents. For many this added to the frustration they already had from having to participate in various meetings and of having several providers in their homes.

There was another WSP who was supposed to be providing Special Needs Community Advocacy and Support (SNCAS) to two of my clients. SNCAS is a service for children/teens who are having a difficult time adjusting and/or performing well academically within their school. The service is designed to help identify any areas where needs are, and to provide the proper supports and services for the children/teens to academically succeed. However, I had a WSP who had been working with two siblings and hadn't been making the most of time during her school visits. She had made several visits but hadn't met with or scheduled a meeting with either of the sibling's teachers, nor had she provided any support to the foster parents. If she had, she would have found out that one of the siblings was in jeopardy of repeating the fourth grade. Yet, during one of my school visits I was able to get this update from the teacher along with getting the teacher's contact information and availability to meet during the week. Even though the WSP had been hired to be the school advocate, she wasn't asking questions that would help this child, nor was she linking the foster parent to supports within the school that could help this child. On one occasion, I remember asking the WSP if the increase of services requested during the last Individual Education Plan (IEP) meeting was benefiting the siblings. Yet, she couldn't tell me if there had been any positive changes in the months following the increase in services. It came to a point where I had to devise a list of questions that she should ask in order to help determine if the child was receiving the right types of school supports. There had been numerous emails sent to her supervisor and just as many discussions with my supervisor, yet no one seemed to do anything until the foster mother stated that she no longer wanted to work with the WSP.

The other factor is that many of the WSPs aren't qualified to provide all of the services listed on the client's IHP so there are times when the child/youth will get anywhere between two and three different WSPs working with them. Not only is this a challenge for the child/youth to keep up with, but the parents also have to keep appointments and have three different people in their homes and/or contacting them via phone. For HCIs it's also frustrating because we have our monthly contacts with each WSP and have to keep documentation on every contact.

Endless meetings and trainings

Like the endless cycle of paperwork, there are tons of meetings and required trainings that we have to attend. Before clients are officially transferred to us we are given their names and their charts to review and told to coordinate with the current health care integrator (HCI) to schedule the transfer meeting. The transfer meeting has to be held for each of the clients who are being transferred. The purpose of this meeting is to discuss the client's background, current living situation, reason for being enrolled in the program along with their progress and/or any difficulties standing in the way of them achieving the goals set. In order to discuss things internally, this meeting is often done in two parts. The first meeting includes the HCI, HCI supervisor(s), and the WSP manager. The second part of this meeting included the HCI transferring the client, the prospective HCI, the HCI supervisors if they were available, along with the case planner or case worker from the foster care agency. Following those two meetings, the HCI and the prospective HCI conduct the home visit with the client, typically within the foster home. If the client and his/her medical consenter and foster parents feel comfortable with the prospective HCI, the medical consenter has to sign a Change of Provider form giving permission for the new HCI to begin work with the client. Following this visit the second contact with the client has to be scheduled, either at the home or somewhere within the community.

When I first started working with this program, I received four transfers within two and half weeks and had to attend all three of those meetings for each client transferred to me. During the same time that I had those transfers take place, I also had to attend a two-day orientation along with a two-day computer training class. Within the first three months of working with the program I was also required to attend a Medicaid training, a separate three-day child welfare training, followed by another mandatory two-day Office of Children and Family Services (OCFS) training. After those trainings, there were other trainings that new hires were told we had to attend within the Bronx office, including trainings for time management, and providing play therapy. While the topics discussed were at times helpful, the mandatory meetings often felt overwhelming for workers just getting familiar with a new work environment and policies. Additionally, becoming familiar with the required paperwork that needed to be completed and of course meeting new families was also no simple task.

In addition to those trainings there were weekly meetings at the Bronx office that included a program meeting followed by a team meeting. When I first started to work for the agency, the Bronx and the Queens units all met at the Bronx office. So social workers who worked from the Queens office had to travel to the Bronx every other week for the program meetings. At the time my supervisor thought it would be fair to hold the team meetings following the program meetings so that the team members from the Queens office wouldn't have to travel to the Bronx for the team meeting the following week. So for the first couple of months I worked for the agency, my Monday mornings consisted of meetings. The program meetings ranged from an hour and a half to two hours depending on the topics discussed and the number of people who felt they needed to voice their concerns during these meetings. Like many of the requirements within the program it didn't stop there. Not including the two monthly contacts required for each client, there could be another one to three client meetings within a three-month period for each client.

For first-year clients we had the Preliminary Meeting, followed by the Initial Meeting if clients were enrolled in the program. After the Initial Meeting there were two quarterly meetings and before the enrollment year was up, the Reauthorization Meeting. After the first year, clients were required to have a Bi-annual Meeting and a Reauthorization Meeting. However, if clients were having a difficult time within their foster homes and had been removed from a foster home, we were often asked by our supervisors to attend a case conference about the client and/or family. So the worker was instructed to type up a summary including the background information of the client, and to prepare a presentation about the problems. The case conference included supervisors, managers, the program director, and the unit director. While I understood the importance of having case conferences, even my supervisor expressed to me how uneasy they made her feel. Since she had started her position around the same time that I started mine, she often confided in me what she felt about these presentations among other issues that she had with the program. On one occasion she in fact expressed that case presentations often turned into a meeting where the health care integrators (HCIs) and at times HCI supervisors would have to defend why something was or wasn't done and listen to how the other HCIs and HCI supervisors would have handled the situation differently.

Yet, regardless of how soon you begin working at the agency all workers had to present and new workers were often volunteered by supervisors during the program meetings to present. This was especially likely if one of the children had been hospitalized or was sent to a different foster home. For us new workers who were on our six-month probation period, the pressure to please our superiors was immense. I mean, there you are in a meeting in front of your co-workers, supervisors and the directors of the program and you're being asked to present during the next case conference. Unless there was some required training that was being held on that day and time, there seemed to be no way to turn down the presentation.

It was difficult enough having your clients in situations that resulted in them being hospitalized or removed from a foster home. We of course had to ensure that they were getting plenty of support during this time. Additionally, for hospitalizations this entailed two required meetings depending on their stay within the hospital, a 10 and at times a 20-Day Hospital Meeting. Once again, the HCI had to coordinate with the HCI supervisor, the case planning team from the foster care agency and of course this time with the hospital staff to discuss how the client was doing, treatment goals, updates regarding medication, and discharge plans. So even though coordinating and participating kept my hands full, I still had to juggle those meetings while preparing for and presenting at the case conference(s). Of course there was also the required documentation that went along with each of the meetings, which not only included progress notes, but the Serious Reportable Incident (SRI) form and Client Change form. The SRI needed to be completed within 48 hours of the incident and had to include updates as they came. Even when the status didn't change, there were separate forms for the SRI progress reports. The Client Change form had to be completed any time the client was out of their foster home. Along with these reports, the HCI also had to write the Service Summary notes from the individual meetings with the clients. Even though waiver service providers couldn't provide services to the children when they were hospitalized, the HCI continued to provide the Health Care Integration service.

In addition to those meetings, there were chart reviews that all workers regardless of how new they were to the agency were subject to participate in. The chart reviews were conducted by representatives from the Office of Children and Family Services (OCFS). We were supposed to be notified two weeks before the chart review to inform us that an audit would be done and for which months the review would be of. However, during my third month working with the program I was only given one week to prepare. According to my supervisor, who was also new to the program, she wasn't aware of one of my charts being reviewed and therefore couldn't provide me with more time to prepare.

While having a client's chart reviewed may not seem like a big deal, once again the pressure is on. Before you even enter that meeting there is a painstaking process of going through the chart with a fine tooth comb to make sure that all of the documentation is filed away and of course in the appropriate area of the chart. The other time consuming part of this process is that if documents like Detailed Service Plans or Individualized Health Plans are missing, the current HCI has to identify what is missing and from which period, and then reach out to the previous waiver service providers or their supervisors to get copies of the document(s).

If the WSP didn't complete the document(s) in question, which happens more often than one would expect, the WSP is asked to complete the document(s) in time for the review. If the WSP no longer works for the program, the WSP manager is instead required to write the document(s) on their behalf. I found it interesting that despite who the health care integrator was during the time that the review was of, that the current HCI had to participate in the chart review meeting to defend things like why documents were missing and/or why clients didn't receive services during the time being reviewed. I could understand this if the HCI was no longer working for the program, but there would be times when the HCI had transferred the client but had remained with the program, just at a different office.

Yet, the responsibility of going through the chart to make sure that the documents were there, in the correct order, along with having to track people down to get staff to write these documents was the responsibility of the current HCI. This didn't seem logical to me, since it was more time consuming for the current HCI to look through a year's worth of notes and documents about services that they hadn't been present for. Yet, there was a HCI who was more knowledgeable about the concerns for the period under review who wasn't required to attend the chart review despite still working for the program.

Wasted travel time

While I will admit that travelling to and from school visits and home visits at times gave me a mini-break from the endless paperwork and phone calls, there were times that I felt bothered by the amount of time it took to travel to some of these visits. Since two of my clients lived within the Bronx, travelling to their homes only took an hour each way. However, for some of my other visits outside the Bronx, I found myself going completely out of the way. Even though I worked out of the Bronx office, I still had clients who lived in Queens and Brooklyn. Wherever my clients lived I had to continue my visits. So from every foster home they resided in, to the hospitalizations deep in Queens, no matter where, I had to continue my visits.

Not only was travelling time consuming, it was also exhausting. I can remember having to visit two brothers I worked with in Queens which took me two hours each way for each visit. Not only did I have to switch from the 2 or 5 train from the Bronx to Manhattan, but once in Manhattan I had to take the E train to the last stop, plus a bus to the last stop. I couldn't understand why I would be assigned to work with children from Queens when we had a Queens office and available HCIs at that office. In fact, one of the siblings who lived in Queens had actually been transferred to me from a Queens HCI. Since I had been assigned to work with his brother, they felt it would make sense to have him transferred to me. Yet, in my opinion it would have made more sense for them to do it the other way around. So needless to say this didn't appear logical to me, nor did it make sense to the foster mother. I wasn't the only worker who had experienced this and after our complaints to our supervisor, months later something was done. However, by the time the transfer took place again, the boys had developed a bond with me. Additionally, their biological mother and foster mother had also become very comfortable working with me. So when they learned that another transfer would take place to transfer the boys back to a Queens HCI, they became angry. Both parents were hesitant and expressed their uneasiness with the boys having to say goodbye to me and start over with a new HCI. This was especially frustrating for the family, since the first HCI from the Queens office was no longer available to accept additional clients. Even though the transfer took place, following the transfer the foster mother started to become resistant to home visits with the new HCI.

Chapter Seventeen

Guilt Over Envy

Something that is rarely ever taken serious is the frustration and sometimes resentment that some social workers have about getting benefits for their clients that they wish they could qualify for. Even though we obviously don't look at the foster children and say "I wish I had their life," there are certain benefits for those foster parents who don't work but receive other government funding that at times drove me crazy. For me, this feeling was very conflicting and uncomfortable. On one hand helping people in need is what got me into social work, but on the other hand after working so hard to finish graduate school and taking out several loans to pay for school, the last thing that I thought was that I would be struggling to get by. Before becoming a social worker I knew approximately how much I would make, and I definitely didn't expect to be rich. However, I also figured that I would earn enough to afford a decent place to live, pay my bills, save a bit and perhaps have some money to hang out with friends. Basically I figured I would be able to do more than just survive and anticipate my next paycheck. I had once figured that I would be able to enjoy the life that I had worked so hard and made sacrifices to have. Yet I found myself worrying about where I could afford to live, what roommate I would have to put up with, and constantly deferring my loan payments just so I could have some money to spend on toiletries and some form of entertainment within the city. Yet like me, there are plenty of other social workers and child welfare workers who make little money; many make just over the amount that would make us eligible for government support. While many social workers and child welfare workers struggle to stretch their paychecks, we are constantly seeing the people we serve receive benefits that range from free metro cards and money for daycare to subsidized housing, food stamps, and even the payment of some utility bills.

At my first job out of graduate school I worked for a non-profit organization as a case planner in a preventive program within a well-known agency. The program I worked for was designed to keep families together by linking them to services needed as well as providing family therapy. During our lunch break, among the discussions of how mentally drained we were, we often discussed how we wished that we either made more money or how we wished that we could qualify for some of the services that we advocated for our clients to get. Some of us would jokingly say that we wished that our rent was paid for us or that we didn't have to worry about spending our money on groceries, but under each of our laughs was quite a bit of seriousness. Yet I couldn't help but feel strange for having those thoughts and feelings. Feelings that made me feel conflicted about whether or not I should be entertaining those thoughts.

Chapter Eighteen

Going Into Some of the Most Hostile and Dangerous Situations Alone

While I have been fortunate enough to avoid any threats and physical harm, there were definitely times that I feared for my safety. I mean, here I was alone, without any protection, and yet I had to make home visits in some of the most impoverished neighborhoods where criminal activity was no stranger. Meanwhile, the police officers who walked through the neighborhoods had a partner and weapons at their disposal. Yet, as social workers we are expected to at times make night visits, go into neighborhoods where no one knows us or probably even cares enough if something happened to us. They at times probably even group us all together and figure that we are all part of the same system that only seeks to take kids away from their families. Nonetheless, we make our visits and learn how to pay close attention to our surroundings while we can't help but feel anxious.

Despite the fact that I grew up in some difficult areas and had been in dangerous situations growing up, going into unfamiliar neighborhoods as a social worker still bothers me. As a kid, regardless of the neighborhoods I lived in, there was still comfort in knowing that the people in those neighborhoods knew me. Yet, despite my feelings and the stress that I experienced, I tried to push those feelings under the surface. I had on some level grown accustomed to how much I stood out in my clients' neighborhoods when I went on home visits. Perhaps my previous job as a case planner had also prepared me for this.

I can remember accompanying a client to court after her husband physically abused her. Due to the domestic violence charge he could only see his children during supervised visits. The first time that I met him he came across as a hostile and threatening person. He was even aggressive during the supervised visits with his children at the agency. It also seemed that he resented the fact that my supervisor and I needed to be present when he got to see his children. So when my supervisor and I accompanied his wife to family court, he continued to show his aggression. The way he looked at my supervisor and me made both of us uncomfortable about what he was capable of doing when we left court. In fact, my supervisor felt so fearful that she asked if I could return to the office with her so that she could get her car out of the parking lot. It was times like this or times like when I had to continue my home visits after having to make a call to report domestic violence against a woman and her nine year-old daughter. It was a no brainer that I would have to call after the woman admitted that her boyfriend attacked her and was responsible for giving her daughter a black eye. Still, it was also frightening when I had to continue making home visits following the call. However, like listening to the frustrations expressed by some of the foster parents, I learned that going into dangerous situations was just another part of my job.

Still, at my last job I couldn't help but at times wonder if a foster parent would have someone in their neighborhood cause trouble for me on my way to the visit. I mainly thought of this when I thought of Desiree's foster mother Ms. Grant, since I knew how much she seemed to want to get rid of me. While I knew that Ms. Grant's frustration was based on her not wanting to be involved with the program, I never knew how far she might go. Still, I had to walk deep into the housing projects where she and Desiree lived and try as hard as I could to hide the concerns I had. Adding to those concerns, my visits with Desiree of course had to be held after Desiree finished school. This was due to her behavioral specialist often meeting Desiree at school for two or three out of her four mandated visits per month. With the frequency that the behavioral specialist visited Desiree at school, coupled with the fact that school visits made Desiree uncomfortable, school visits weren't a likely option for me. While this wasn't much of an issue during the spring and summer months, during the fall and winter evenings I became very conscious of what could happen on my way to or from those visits.

Other times there were more obvious situations that made my anxiety level shoot through the roof and only added to the other parts of this work that caused me to feel stressed; like during my first meetings with Cari's mother Ms. Mead in which her mother was all over the place. Ms. Mead was loud, aggressive and unpredictable. She was also very angry and often expressed that she felt that the foster care agency wasn't doing anything to help her or Cari. At times it felt like she grouped us all together, and when she started to pace through the apartment I wasn't sure what she would do. These were the types of situations that I had to emotionally prepare myself for when I made visits, despite how nerve-wracking it all made me feel inside.

Chapter Nineteen

Being on Call 24 Hours a Day, 7 Days a Week

Another factor that added to the emotional drain was the fact that this particular job required that the social workers carry a mobile phone 24 hours a day, 7 days a week. So even if we had just gotten home from an exhausting day of meetings at the office and home visits throughout the city, we also had to be on the job after hours. There was no breathing room and certainly always a feeling that I had to be prepared to drop whatever I was doing. There would be times when I was out with my friends or with a significant other, but if I received a call about a child getting into an argument with a foster parent, getting into trouble at school and or running away from home, I would have to take the call. Additionally, I would suddenly have to be available for a number of calls that needed to be made. Being on call at times felt like having a part-time job on top of my full-time position.

I remember in one of the program meetings we had, there was a discussion and demonstration about how we should handle the after-hours calls. We were told that if the family called the health care integrator (HCI), the HCI would have to first get information about the incident, provide support to the family over the phone, and then inform the family that the crisis waiver service provider (WSP) would be calling to provide additional support over the phone or in person if needed. So the HCI would then call the WSP to provide this person with the information about the incident and have them reach out to the family. Then the HCI would have to call the HCI supervisor and re-explain to the supervisor what had just occurred and ask if anything else should be done. If the HCI supervisor had recommendations that weren't initially thought of by the HCI, then the HCI would have to call the family and/or the WSP to provide these recommendations. In the meantime the HCI supervisor would have to notify his/her supervisor of the incident.

Following implementation of crisis support to the foster child/youth and/or family, the WSP would have to call their supervisor, the WSP manager, and do the same thing that the HCI and HCI supervisor had to do with their supervisor. If the authorities needed to be involved, they would also call to obtain additional information about the incident and your relationship to the child/youth. Of course it would never end there because when we returned to the office, we had to type up the Serious Reportable Incident form and email this to our supervisor. If there were things that needed to be added to this form, the HCI supervisor would send the form back to the HCI for revisions. While the reports were being made, there was constant follow-up. Since one child could have up to three WSPs, the HCI had to notify the WSP(s) and provide updates to each. The HCI also had to discuss the incident with the case planner and/or case worker form the foster care agency. Of course each of those conversations including the contacts with the child/youth and foster parent had to be written in progress notes and entered into the computer system Connections.

Even when there weren't incidents that warranted immediate attention, we could receive a phone call from a parent venting about some aspect of the services that they weren't pleased with, including any dissatisfaction with WSPs. I remember having one foster parent in particular who nearly every week felt that she needed to give me a call in the evening to complain about something. So she spent nearly 45 minutes going on and on about how little support she felt she was receiving from this particular waiver service provider. Since this particular foster parent worked during the day, most of the calls took place when I was looking to unwind from my day of work. Even though I wanted to ignore those evening calls, I knew that it was part of my job to be available 24 hours a day, 7 days a week.

Chapter Twenty

Feeling the Pressure Everywhere and Wanting to Break Free

I soon found myself dreading going to work and noticed that I started to get chest pains when Sunday evening came around. It was something about physically having to be present at that job that made me feel sick. I could no longer hide the feelings that I had tried so hard to suppress. Not even the individual therapy I had entered again during this period seemed to help. It became evident to me that while it was partially due to the nature of this work, it was even more frustrating working within a system that made me feel powerless to change it. While I had expressed my feelings to my colleagues, many of whom felt the same way, no one seemed to feel that they could change the way things were. We had all gotten similar stories from our supervisors who, even though they understood how ridiculous the paperwork was or how grueling being on call 24 hours/7 days a week was, didn't see any relief of these requirements for the future. My supervisor often said that based on her meetings with representatives from the office that monitored and set the requirements for our program, the plan was to make the paperwork and requirements even more demanding. So it seemed that there was no light at the end of the tunnel.

Something else that disturbed me was that our agency only sent two representatives to speak on behalf of the other workers for the program. Yet the two people who were sent to the conference upstate included a supervisor who had recently started working for the program along with a waiver service provider manager. None of the health care integrators or even the waiver service providers was invited to participate. However, we were the people who had to meet with the children and families in the field regularly. We were also the ones who had to write the bulk of the required documents, yet we weren't invited to have a say about how the program could be improved. I couldn't understand how they would choose two people who were so removed from the daily work in the field or from having to write the reports to represent us. This only added to my annoyance with the illogical manner and disrespectful way in which the workers were treated.

During lunch my co-workers and I discussed our frustration, and how we could try to change things. At times we spoke of discussing this during the union meetings. However, our fellow health care integrator and office union representative felt just as pessimistic about changes taking place through this route. She often expressed that when workers had expressed their feelings in the past, they were often penalized in some way later on. Either the supervisor would constantly be checking every detail of their work and constantly requesting changes, or the HCI would all of a sudden have chart reviews more frequently than other workers. She felt so frustrated about being at the agency that she continually confided in me that she was looking for a different job.

Being promoted within the program didn't seem like something that most of us wanted. While it meant that there was less writing including that of progress notes, IHPs, DSPs, SSFs, CANS, SRIs, CCFs, and the other documents required, there were other demands that took too much of a toll. Being a supervisor meant that you would have to edit all of the notes and reports from health care integrators (HCIs), unless a HCI was on vacation or left the agency. At that time, the HCI supervisor would actually have to write the notes and reports regarding client updates and visits. Other than that, supervisors have the same number of meetings, if not more staff meetings, they have to attend daily. Plus, they often have to accompany the HCIs during the team meetings like Preliminary, Initial, Quarterly, Bi-annual, Reauthorization, and Hospital Meetings. Like us, they also have to join committees when there are program events like picnics and parties held for clients and holiday staff celebrations. Supervisors are also often involved in organizing other office events for staff including bridal and baby showers. So between everything else, very few of us aspired to become a supervisor within this program.

So we often talked about how much we wanted to leave. This was very common among the social workers within this program, especially those who were licensed master social workers. The social workers who weren't licensed often expressed that they felt trapped because they couldn't find other positions without their license that would pay the same salary. It was hard enough to make it on their current salary, so they couldn't bear going to another job only to make less. This was particularly hard for those social workers who had a child or children that they needed to care for.

Even for those of us who were licensed social workers, we often discussed how similar this could be at other positions based on the current state of the child welfare system. Also, most of the jobs for licensed master social workers (LMSWs) in the area of child welfare are very similar. For those who want to practice in the mental health area of the field, there has been a shift in the profession now requiring that a great number of these positions be filled by a licensed clinical social worker (LCSW). In order to earn the credentials for the LCSW, there are several steps that need to be taken. In addition to having received a Master's degree in social work, you are required to work in a clinical setting under the supervision of a LCSW. During this time you must earn the specified hours required within a clinical setting along with earning clinical hours in supervision with a LCSW as your supervisor. The second requirement is to pass the licensing exam similar to the exam for earning the credentials of a LMSW, but consisting of questions focusing on clinical work. However, over the past years the types of jobs in which social workers can earn clinical hours have become more limited. Unfortunately, the way in which the program I worked for is set up, the social workers can't earn clinical hours. Additionally, the program doesn't require that the supervisors are LCSW. Therefore the current supervisors wouldn't be able to provide the clinical supervision required for the LCSW credentials. And therefore the program would have to hire licensed clinical social workers to provide clinical supervision.

Additionally, as the program is currently set up, the work that the health care integrators (HCIs) provide isn't considered clinical work, even though the Individualized Health Plans are considered clinical documents. Yet, instead of allowing the HCIs/social workers to do the clinical work with the clients, they instead have to rely on the waiver services providers (WSPs) to implement the clinical work. So for services including the Family/Caregiver Supports and Services, which is very similar to the type of work done during family therapy, this is done by a WSP. Yet this service along with others, like Crisis Avoidance Management and Training, can be devised and implemented in a way that is clinical. Instead, these services are provided by WSPs most of whom only have undergraduate degrees and who don't necessarily have degrees in social work or psychology. So instead of allowing the social workers an opportunity to advance by allowing them to implement the work that they write treatment plans for, the work is often done by those who don't have the same level of expertise and experience. I have witnessed plenty of health care integrators having to spoon-feed the WSPs on which intervention strategies they should use to implement the services. Yet, we still don't get the clinical hours or credit we deserve for doing this. We instead are told that this is just part of our job.

Even when we meet with the clients to discuss their progress this doesn't count as clinical work. Yet, we have to be responsible for the coordination of these services and constantly monitor the child's progress while also ensuring that the WSPs are doing what is specified in the Individualized Health Plans. If we were allowed to do the work, not only would this mean qualifying to earn clinical hours, but it would also cut down the tremendous amount of time it often takes contacting and coordinating with the WSPs to check the progress of our clients. It would also save a great deal of time on the documentation because the HCI would only have to focus on documenting their work with the client and wouldn't have to be bothered by the additional reporting from contacts with WSPs. Instead, the program currently operates with endless paperwork and a web of phone calls and emails required to discuss updates and fulfill the monthly mandated contacts.

Most of this could be a lot simpler, beneficial and less costly, yet it continues to be perpetuated in a moronic existence of waste. Not to mention what happens, when the WSPs move on to other jobs after they finish their degrees, or when the foster children/youth move to boroughs that the WSPs aren't willing to travel to. When this happens, the HCIs have to look for new WSPs to work with the children and families. Plus, the children/youth and their parents have to get used to a new WSP or set of WSPs to provide services. This is why most of us just feel like getting out, and why those who have the opportunity to leave end up doing so.

Yet, there is still a feeling of annoyance I experience when I think of how us workers often having to start over somewhere else. It is bothersome when we feel pressured to leave one situation, only to find similar issues within other agencies. Like me, my colleagues talked about how frustrating it was that we social workers often had to drop things and pick up and leave. However, we had worked hard to get there and had started to feel more knowledgeable about how things were, and of course felt bonds with our clients. However, it appeared that we were expected to leave if we didn't like the way things were. In many ways it came across as if we were all disposable. It felt like there was a mentality that a new batch of social workers was right around the corner getting ready to graduate with their ideals, only to have the hard fist of this system crush them. Like my colleagues, I became tired of running and having to give up what we had spent so much time and hard work on. Yet every time I looked around so many of us were gone. Those of us who stayed were so beaten down from the daily grind and busywork that we had very little energy to fight back. It felt as if we were in an abusive relationship where our self-esteem had been beaten down and where we lived in fear of leaving.

Chapter Twenty One

How It Seems Social Workers and Other Child Welfare Workers are Viewed

Adding to what we already experience from the child welfare system are films like *Precious* that make it seem like social workers and other child welfare workers just go into homes, take notes, and leave without doing much to help. While I was deeply moved by watching the movie *Precious* and appreciated how important issues about teen pregnancy and sexual abuse were brought to the forefront, the impression I received of child welfare workers definitely bothered me.

In general, I find that little is discussed about how case workers and social workers in child welfare often have anywhere between six and thirty children and/or families to meet with, monitor, link to services, advocate for, including going to court with, and provide counseling to. Or how we spend a great deal of time completing the endless paperwork for services, attending trainings, attending supervision to better serve our clients, among many other responsibilities and hats that we wear on a daily basis. Yet, there is still a perception that many of us are just there to pass time or to take people's kids away. I have yet to meet a social worker or case worker who has said that they enjoyed having to make reports about any form of abuse happening to a child or to any other client. For me making calls to the State Central Registry was beyond heartbreaking and emotionally trying.

Every time I had to make a call, I was thinking of what it meant for the child and the family; the fear of what would happen if the allegations were so well hidden from the child protective specialist that following the investigation the allegations only made the abuse worse. Or if the child or children were removed from the home, what this meant for them in the months and years to come; if they would be separated from their siblings, or if they would be placed from one foster home to the next until they were sent to a residential treatment facility or group home. Would they become hopeless and cynical about the world even as children? Would they lose their desire to live life if they felt that they had little control over what happened to them? How would they see themselves? Did they blame themselves? When I went home at night, it was often hard to sleep with thoughts like these among other concerns that were on my mind. There were even times that I cried from thinking of conversations I had had with the children I worked with, especially after they were hospitalized for long periods of time or moved to a new foster home after being abused. I have lost count of the many nights of tossing and turning or trying to let some TV show help me escape until I fell asleep.

Chapter Twenty Two

Still No Walk in the Park

Yet no matter how I try to tune out what I have seen and experienced as a social worker within the child welfare system, there is little that can completely help me escape the darkness of it. So I turned to writing, as I had done during my adolescence in hopes that I could make some sense of what I had seen and been through. However, I can't say that I expected where writing down my thoughts would lead me. Yet writing this book forced me to face the injustice of this system, and in doing so has helped me to face my past and the journey that led me back to the world of foster care. Like anyone else, who I have become and my life in general is a work in progress.

There are in fact several things that I continue to struggle with despite the many years I have spent receiving therapy to gain insight and to learn coping skills. There are still times when I cry because I want my father to show that he cares. Yet still I continue to go on. Just as I continue to live with how my sister resents the relationship that my brother and I had with our mother and therefore continues to stay away from us despite our many attempts to have a relationship with her. I still wake up hoping that my mother will finally beat her dependency on drugs as she tries to forget the past and numb her pain. I still try to keep some hope alive that she will no longer feel that she is to blame for Darren sexually abusing me. I desperately want her to see how special she is to me, and how much I appreciate the wonderful things that she has done over the years. I want her to know how proud I am of her for earning her college degree. I also greatly admire how after graduating from college, she later became a case worker within the child welfare system. Or how I appreciated her buying me a laptop during my second year of college, or how she provided me with money to open my first checking account. The list could go on and on, but she still struggles to see how important she has been and will continue to be in my life. I hold on to the hope of seeing the day that she will no longer need to hide from the pain of our past, but instead take the time to learn and grow from it. Just as I continue to hold on to the belief that the soldiers of the foster care system will get the due respect and support to fight the battles that need to be fought for change.

I hold on tight to the belief that children in foster care will have the opportunities to live their lives without the fear of foster parents who don't see beyond the money, and that they will have the chance to experience their childhoods without the myriad of mental health providers and child welfare workers all working with them at the same time. I instead envision a time when foster children can participate in programs that help support the growth of their minds and that support them in building healthy self-esteem needed for them to thrive within this society. It is my hope that this book will spark the needed conversations about the current state of the foster care system and set plans in motion to work towards providing the type of environment for foster kids that we would all want our own children to grow up in.

www.ingramcontent.com/pod-product-compliance
Lightning Source LLC
Chambersburg PA
CBHW022254290526
45785CB00015B/842
* 9 7 8 1 4 7 5 9 4 6 9 3 2 *